After the panic

After the panic

Surviving bad investments and bad advice

Gareth Morgan
with John McCrystal

PiP
PUBLIC
INTEREST
PUBLISHING

To the thousands of New Zealanders who have lost their life's savings in the finance industry debacle of the naughty Noughties — the period since 2007. Legal recourse may be beyond your means but that does not mean that those who did it are innocent. Far from it in fact, and I hope this book goes some way to sheeting accountability home to an industry that has much to do to regain the respect of ordinary people.

A catalogue record for this book is available from the National Library of New Zealand

First published 2009. Reprinted 2009.

© 2009 Gareth Morgan

The moral rights of the author have been asserted

ISBN 978 0 473 15204 8

Design: IslandBridge
Cover design: Nick Turzynski
Author photograph: Chris Coad

Printed in New Zealand by McCollams

McCollams uses non-chlorine-bleached papers from sustainably managed forests and vegetable-based, mineral-oil free inks.

Contents

Introduction

Clean up your act when it comes to investing
your savings or it's milk arrowroots & mittens
in Bluff for you.
(Pension Panic, 2006)

In 2006, I published a book named *Pension Panic*. In it, I tried to provide Kiwis with some urgent advice as to how to sort their finances. As the title suggests, *Pension Panic* was a book 'intended to scare you'. It was high time for some salutary scaremongering: there was just too much unjustified complacency about the financial future around, and I wasn't alone in worrying what this collective 'she'll be right' insouciance meant for people's retirement prospects.

Mind you, it was pretty hard to be taken seriously. Things were chugging along. You could get a two-year fixed home loan from TSB for 7.95 per cent. You could place your money in an on-line call account with Kiwibank for an annual return of 7.3 per cent. Or there was a wide range of finance companies to choose from, offering that all-important couple of percentage points more than the banks: Capital + Merchant Finance were offering 9.88 per cent for 18 months. Perhaps your eye might be caught by a coupon in the paper advertising Hanover Finance, the one that the nice former newsreader was endorsing on telly. They were offering 8.75 per cent — doesn't sound too risky — and the newspaper ad featured a picture of that same newsreader overprinted with 'Investing is all about reliability and trust, making a choice you may rely on, year after year'.

But for those looking behind the headlines, all was not well. Of particular concern when I was compiling *Pension Panic* was that:

▷ too many people had placed all their bets on one horse, namely property, and we explained 'why housing's stuffed';

▷ far too much debt had been taken on by households in order to take bets on rising property prices;

▷ those who had faithfully saved in the saving sector's labyrinth of lousy products could be assured of only one thing — the 'rat's nest' that is the New Zealand funds-management industry was guaranteed to provide woeful returns, a conclusion that a survey conducted by *Consumer* magazine also reached;

▷ the range of flash finance company debentures (loans raised from the public for the purposes of on-lending to others, commonly property developers) and mortgage funds was bound to blow up once the property bubble burst, and we would see large swathes of the population financially ruined as a result;

▷ the financial advisory 'profession' was actually just a bunch of door-to-door commission salesmen whose knowledge of the investment strategy behind the products they were flogging was minimal. Their sole focus was the commissions that the issuers of these products paid out to those who placed them, meaning 'advisors' had no scruples about piling mum-and-dad investors into toxic products to get those payments.

Of late, the combination of weakening investor markets and exposure of finance-sector frauds has led to vast tracts of personal wealth being laid to waste, and the wider economic ramifications due to the sheer size of the financial-sector collapse has triggered the elimination of jobs, leaving many who dreamed of retirement just around the corner instead contemplating more years of wearily trudging to work, followed by a life of dry biscuits in Bluff.

After the Panic is the latest in a series of books intended to raise the financial literacy of the New Zealand public, and to help you help yourself as you pick your way through the debris that the global panic has strewn across the landscape.

One of the most important points that this book will seek to make is that what we're seeing is not just a financial and economic downturn; it is finally exposing an epidemic of behaviour from members of the financial sector that's long been contrary to the public interest. Drain the swamp, and all manner of unsightly objects come into view. In a softening market, it's a lot harder to hide unethical or incompetent practices or downright swindling, and the sheer scale of the wrongs wrought should sound a warning to savers and investors in the future.

The following litany of lapses in financial-sector competence (by no means exhaustive) gives you a taste of the type of deleterious dealing to the public from players on our local investment scene:

▷ June 2006 — Provincial Finance goes into receivership, despite public-seducing celebrity endorsement.

▷ July 2007 —Bridgecorp receivership. Director Rod Petricevic — a serial finance company bankrupt whose infamy was first confirmed during the Euro-National debacle of the 1980s — is caught out once again misrepresenting his offering to a gullible public.

▷ March 2008 — ANZ National Bank promotes a high-risk fund to its innocent savers as a low-to-moderate risk, near-cash alternative. The fund, run by ING, suspends withdrawals in March 2008. Chairman Dryden Spring, chief executive Graham Hodges.

▷ March 2008 — ING prohibits investors from cashing out from several of its fixed-interest, conservative and moderate-risk funds. In reality, the funds were invested in too many poor-quality assets. Chief executive Marc Lieberman.

▷ By May 2008 financial planning group Vestar, owned by Australian company MFS Group, has been decimated and sold on. Vestar's loan book was largely with parties related to MFS Group (Cymbis,

Boston), at least one of which had solicited a credit rating and then quietly suppressed it when the rating told the brutal truth. Other ill-considered investments included Bridgecorp.

▷ October 2008 — ING (Netherlands), one of New Zealand's largest fund managers requires government rescue, despite having promoted themselves on their solidity and dependability right up to the day they went cap-in-hand to the Dutch government.

▷ June 2008 — Dominion Finance receivership. Directors include Vance Arkinstall, chief executive of the Investment, Savings and Insurance Association, a lobby group funded by insurance multinationals to influence New Zealand's financial market regulators.

▷ June 2008 — Hanover Finance moratorium, despite celebrity endorsement from newsreader Richard Long. Large tracts of the lending is to related parties on questionable commercial terms (delayed interest payments), although the nature of these 'friendly' terms wasn't made clear to those sucked in by the fund-raising ads to the public. Co-owners (who extracted large dividends from the company just before its collapse) Eric Watson and Mark Hotchin.

▷ . . . and there are dozens more; this is no more than a sampler. We will cover some more in the book and list some more names of the friendly folk behind the apocalypse in the appendix.

The hall of shame is pretty crowded and it has become a tradition in the finance sector that those responsible for what is in my view harmful behaviour hide behind corporate acronyms, change company names as soon as bad press accumulates, and readily form new companies once their previous one has run aground. None of this type of behaviour, where personal accountability seems to be nowhere near top-of-mind of the perpetrators of these acts, is in the public interest. Yet regulators are tardy, to put it mildly, to help the public identify the perpetrators. And it's not just finance companies, the financial advisors who sell the shonky products that fleece their clients don't leave the industry. They merely duck under cover for a while, to reappear in due course in other houses.

In my opinion incompetent and devious behaviour among those charged with the guardianship of the public's savings is widespread within the New Zealand finance community and rooting it out and naming the individuals involved is well overdue. It's people who do these deeds, not inert company logos, and for the victims (at least) naming and shaming of the people responsible is part of natural justice.

In this book, I'll tell you why I think the New Zealand savings and investment sector remains structurally sick, why the regulators just don't get it, what the global financial-sector-led recession means for a successful personal savings and investment strategy from here on, and finally how best you can navigate the investment cycle ahead — all the while avoiding the traps big-brand, multinational banks and insurance companies set in your path, not to mention what I consider to be the blandishments of some deceiving finance companies and the unscrupulous double-dealing of financial advisors.

There are two parts to the story. In chapters 1 through to 4 of the book, I'll have a look at the macroeconomics of the present crisis — the fundamental, structural problems that gave rise to it, and that have fostered the types of abuses I'll discuss in the latter portion, namely the rapaciousness of the savings and finance sector. Then I'll finish with some advice for both regulators — who need to wake up — and for savers trying to get back on their feet.

Here's the plan. The first couple of chapters look at how the global recession was triggered, the consequences for a highly indebted economy like New Zealand's, and how economic recovery might finally emerge. An important theme of the book is the centrality of what we'll call 'fast-and-loose credit' to so much of what has been going on. Part of this is the pivotal role played by lax central banking in causing the boom-and-bust through its pursuit of economic growth at all costs — no matter how unsustainable — usually by loosening the purse strings.

In Chapter 3, I consider why, if sustainable economic growth is so hard to achieve, do we bother? Is it a rational alternative for us as a country to sit back, relax and let the rest of the world go by? Would we be happier? After all, our income levels continue to fall down the OECD listings despite efforts to work harder. Maybe it's just not something we do well. Like the Swiss, we do far better at yachting than growing our income.

In Chapter 4, the last of the economic overview, I reiterate that it's not because we can't save enough to save ourselves, but rather what we've done with our savings that has landed us where we are today. Either we've been to the casino and put all our chips on the perpetual boom in property, or we've handed our hard-won savings over to those who, in my opinion, have no respect whatsoever for the fiduciary duty of care they owe us as guardians of our property.

Chapters 5 through 7 consider why things are so bad in the savings and investment sector, why levels of competence are so low that you'd be better picking what shares to buy by throwing darts at the world share-market board yourself. We see just how the financial services industry is structured to abuse the rights of individual savers, and compile a list of differences between the elements of good portfolio practice and what they actually do with your money.

Then, in Chapter 8, I get down and dirty and take apart some of the portfolios we have seen from financial planners practising in New Zealand, revealing in my opinion just what destruction they have wrought on their clients. Chapter 9 shows why remedial regulatory responses to the financial-sector 'swine flu' are so inadequate, and just how self-serving the funds-management industry is.

Chapter 10 is for the regulators — showing them how to get out of bed in the morning, go to work and actually add value in the public interest, rather than show such cowardice under fire from finance-sector lobbyists. In Chapter 11, I return to the long-suffering saver/investor and provide some specific advice as to how to set about building your store of wealth in these troubled times, so that you can enjoy a greater range of choices. After all, time is the only truly non-renewable resource each of us has.

Finally, in the Appendix there's a list of individual directors of failed finance companies. It's about accountability. We'll also include some of the more memorable quotations from their solicitations to the saving public, which will leave a sour taste for many a year to come.

1

What happened and why?

You may have noticed that the world's financial system is in a colossal mess right at the moment.

In order to understand how we might get out of this mess and to understand what the brave new financial and economic world we'll be living in afterwards will look like, we need to have a look at how we got here in the first place.

Financial markets and global and national economies all have their ups and downs. Seasoned investors and anyone who is in a business of any description is well accustomed to taking the rough with the smooth. The recommended strategy — particularly when trading in volatile markets where the ride can be a little hairier — is to sit tight in the bad times and await the good.

There are plenty of people who see the present global situation as just another slowdown, inevitable after the well-deserved boom we were all enjoying, and that's all there is to it. Just hold on, this point of view urges, and things will soon be back to 'normal'.

As appealing as this Pollyanna-ish view of the credit crunch recession may be, if ever there was an economic pitfall different to the trifling potholes we've experienced over the last 20 years or so, this is it. A prompt resumption of 'normal transmission' would be a fine thing, but the collapse of many of the world's largest financial institutions suggests that we ought not hold our breath until it occurs.

Securitisation: the straw that broke the financial sector's back

One of the most fascinating aspects of the dizzying worldwide credit expansion of the 10 years between 1997 and 2007 was the mythology that market players and analysts indulged in to justify it, and to suggest that this was an endless summer, a 'new era'. The bottomless well of borrowings into which everyone was dipping wasn't inflationary, you heard people say, because it was all based on productivity gains that were quite without precedent, made possible by spectacular advances in information technologies and the cheaper production of goods (mainly in China) unleashed by globalisation. Thanks to this fortuitous combination of factors, it was argued, the old rules somehow didn't apply.

It turns out they did apply after all. One final straw was added to the credit camel's back and the whole unrealistic and unsustainable thing collapsed in late 2007.

That last straw was the implosion of the so-called 'subprime' mortgage market in the United States, which spread to wider investment markets and plunged the world into a long-overdue recession. The means by which the virus afflicting the dodgy end of the US home loans market jumped species and ravaged the wider financial system was the practice known as 'securitisation'.

Once upon a time, banks were in the business of being 'portfolio lenders'. They raised money (mostly) from depositors, and loaned money to people who could afford a (substantial) deposit on a house, accepting repayment over a long term of 20, 25 or even 30 years. It was all very orderly, and it was subject to the regulation of the international banking code, the Basel Accord on Banking Supervision, which charged central banks with ensuring that lending institutions retained sufficient capital reserves to honour their commitments should the loans on their books turn sour.

Trouble was, after World War II and particularly in the United States, there just wasn't enough money in the banking system to meet the demand for home loans — until it occurred to some bright spark that the loans on a bank's book represented an asset that could itself be used as collateral to raise funds from investors, long before any of those loans were due to mature. Instead of waiting for 10 loans of $100,000 apiece to mature in 25 years' time, say, a bank could pool those loans and sell 10 shares (mortgage-backed securities) to investors at $100,000 apiece. This provided instant gratification for the lender, who would otherwise have had to wait 25 years for full repayment of the funds they had advanced. And while it meant forgoing income from interest that would accrue over that 25-year period, it also meant dodging the risk that any of those 10 borrowers would default on their loan repayments. Similarly, whereas anyone paying $100,000 to take a single loan off the bank's books was 100 per cent exposed if that loan turned dog on them, by purchasing a mortgage-backed security, he or she was only exposed by 10 per cent to any one of the 10 loans in the pool — risk was truly shared.

This is what is meant by the 'secondary mortgage market'. It's the trade in mortgage-backed securities, where loans made to mums and dads toiling away to repay the mortgage on their home are treated as assets. Further, the new security itself could be used as security for capital-raising — in exactly the same way mums and dads use the house they buy as security for the money they borrow from the bank in the first place. Yes, that's right. You could borrow against the loans you had out to other folk!

When it was all chugging along, securitisation was praised by no less a figure than the (then) chairman of the US central bank, Alan Greenspan, for its ability to spread risk across the entire investment community rather than quarantining it in the home loans sector.

And it wasn't just home loans that became subject to securitisation. Other forms of lending suited it far better: loans on automobiles, the second-largest category in the United States after home loans, are for smaller amounts and typically have a much shorter term, and these were next in line. But credit-card debt, insurance and reinsurance contracts, loans to business — it was open season on the lot of them.

Of course, the original lender, having decided to forgo the return from accrual of interest over the term of the loan, needs to make money somewhere. And the source of that income is from service fees charged in extending the loan in the first place. This creates an incentive to go out and lend, lend, lend, packaging up the loans accumulated in these marketing drives and securitising them in order to raise more funds with which to lend, lend, lend, clipping the ticket all the while.

In the US market, there are even opportunities for the original lender to profit from handling the processes that begin once a borrower defaults on their loan if they retain the 'servicing contracts'. But looking into these in any detail will serve only to shake whatever residual faith you may have in man's humanity to man.

Anyone spot the obvious flaw in the securitisation system? Once you've sold the potential reward accruing to the loans in your pool, you've also shifted the risk onto the investors and, more often than not, moved the loan beyond the scrutiny of the central bank that's charged with overseeing how lending is being conducted. Since there's no residual risk for the original lender, there's no incentive whatsoever for the lender to satisfy themselves that they're making a prudent lending decision — that the borrower will be able to service the loan, and that the asset the borrower is offering as security is sufficiently valuable to cover the loan in the event that the borrower defaults.

Freddie and Fannie get hammered

The road to hell, as they say, is paved with good intentions.

Part of the American Dream has always been to own your own home. And due to their benevolence — or their shrewd eye for the political main chance, take your pick — successive United States administrations have worked the world's most powerful economy into an invidious position.

In 1938, in order to assist low-income families into houses as part of his 'New Deal' package, Franklin D Roosevelt set up an agency named the Federal National Mortgage Association. This was privatised in 1968, and acquired as a nickname the friendly, down-home acronym of 'Fanny Mae'. Another, analogous organisation was created to provide competition for Fanny Mae in 1970, the Federal Home Loan Mortgage Corporation (known as 'Freddy Mac'). Both organisations were allowed to securitise their portfolio of home loans, and perhaps driven by the conviction that no US government would allow either of these institutions to fail, their offerings were heavily subscribed by US and overseas investors.

In 1999, Bill Clinton's administration placed enormous pressure on lenders — Freddy and Fanny, as the government's pet lenders, — to make funds available to borrowers who had a chequered credit history, such as: a string of defaults on loan repayments, a record of having difficulties meeting financial obligations, or more serious hiccups such as bankruptcies.

Meanwhile, US administrations were extending all kinds of tax breaks to people with mortgages. This had the predictable effect of ensuring that Americans swiftly borrowed to the hilt against their houses to buy consumer items such as cars, electrical goods and overseas trips. Meanwhile, too, rapidly rising house prices saw people borrowing more and more against the ballooning equity in their homes. It all added up to Americans becoming the most indebted people in the world.

The fire started in the so-called 'subprime' end of the market — the aforementioned underclass of loans extended to people who got mortgages when they shouldn't have had mortgages. The moment house prices softened, the rate of defaulting in the subprime sector of the home loan market soared.

Particularly hard hit in this sudden meltdown were poor old Fanny and Freddy. As soon as the value of their mortgage-backed securities plunged — in spite, it should be noted, of glowing credit ratings extended by naïve or negligent ratings agencies — they were in trouble, and so too were the mortgage-backed offerings of other lenders. People who had borrowed cheap money from banks and invested it in higher-yielding mortgage-backed securities were stuffed. Since no one knew who was exposed to the subprime crash and how badly, there was profound uncertainty over everyone's financial position. Paranoia ruled supreme. Banks grew very reluctant to lend to anyone at all, precipitating what's been called the 'credit crunch crisis'. Without credit providing grist to the economic mills, a recession — and a deep one, at that — became inevitable.

It should all have been a problem that was confined to a few banks who were silly enough to try to help the hopeless into homes. At worst, it should have been an American problem. Trouble was, trading in mortgage-backed securities was a feature of the entire financially sophisticated world, and in a sense, everyone was exposed to the US subprime market. The bad news spread pretty quickly.

The 2008 finance-sector crash, Kiwi-style

In New Zealand, the securitisation-led explosion in lending passed us by for a couple of reasons. We have rather thin and unsophisticated markets, which makes it hard to amass large bundles of repackaged mortgages and sell them off. And the Reserve Bank has a visionary requirement that loan originators must retain a certain capital-backing behind any security issued — they can't just shift the risk *holus bolus* onto investors.

But that's not to say all is well in camp here. The quality of our banks' loan book has deteriorated markedly in recent years, and there has been all but complete carnage in the finance company sector.

Our banks have played fast and loose with depositors' funds, just as they have overseas. Anyone who can cast their mind back just 25 years ago will remember when you needed at least a 30 per cent deposit to buy a house. Those days are long gone, and the modern-day banker — who isn't a real banker at all — will tell you that their lending decisions these days are no longer based so much on the value of the house as on the client's 'ability to service the loan'. In other words, they look at your income, and if that is adequate to service the mortgage, then the bank is happy to lend.

But what happens if you, the borrower, lose your job and your income is ravaged? In modern-day banking, this possibility isn't even contemplated, or at least not seriously — as though phenomena such as recessions have become a thing of the past.

Oh dear. Such a departure from the long-established norm of banking practice was always bound to set up our financial system for a fall. The shift has taken a while, and it has come about as the direct result of the typically modern aversion among central banks to talk of a recession. Before the R word can appear in an op-ed piece in a weekend paper, central banks will have loosened credit conditions in an attempt to head off the prospect of any bad times. In other words, we've become allergic to even the whiff of a no-growth period of economic activity. Never mind that in conventional economics the occasional period of economic malaise is regarded as a healthy thing, and necessary to cleanse the excesses from the system — to get rid of the crappy loans, the weak businesses and to release resources for more productive employment once 'normal transmission resumes'.

So knowing that any given economic slowdown will only run for a short time before the central bank will ride to the rescue by easing credit conditions, lenders have become nonchalant about downturns. They've forgotten how to be afraid — afraid that a downturn might end up being long-lived — and in dismissing any such prospect, they've stopped worrying about the collateral backing of the loans they make. So long as their clients presently have incomes well in excess of their mortgage obligations, what could possibly go wrong? The chances that they might lose their job, default on their mortgage and that the collateral may have to be liquidated — the mortgaged house sold to repay the loan — are regarded as negligible.

Our central bank, the Reserve Bank, seems to have missed this deterioration in the asset-backing of bank lending. In New Zealand, the quality of the banks' lending books has fallen through the floor, as banks have progressively moved from requiring a 30 per cent deposit to (in some cases) waiving the need for borrowers to bring to the table any deposit at all. These loose financing requirements fuelled a property boom, which the government aided and abetted with schemes like 'Welcome Home', whereby Housing New Zealand (that is, the government) lends folk their deposits, ensuring that even those who can't afford a home can buy one.

The irony in New Zealand is that during this international orgy of credit expansion our Reserve Bank has been an active accomplice in the deterioration in the quality of the banking assets (their mortgage loans) that secure depositors' funds.

And meanwhile, of course, the Reserve Bank has completely ignored what has gone on in the netherworld of the shadow banking system, where the finance companies operate. At its best, this is New Zealand's own version of the US subprime-mortgage market — the source of funds for people or businesses whose credit history is too shady for the formal banking sector to lend to. Something resembling securitisation occurs in this kind of company: their initial investment, often in dodgy areas such as property development or automotive loans or poor-quality mortgages, is funded by overseas borrowings and is subsequently offered as security for debentures offered to the public to raise still more capital.

At their worst, finance companies are nothing short of swindlers operating pyramid or Ponzi schemes — the kind of arrangement made infamous by the devious dealings of Bernard L Madoff, who defrauded investors of something like US$50 billion (a Ponzi scheme is one where investors are paid 'interest' on their investment from funds raised from new investors). Too many Kiwi finance companies have been exposed for soliciting investment from the more ignorant or financially illiterate corners of the household market with slick advertising and celebrity endorsements, and then loaning these monies to related parties on totally non-commercial terms. While times are good, and there's plenty of money pouring in from the greedy and the gullible who can't see past the attractive interest rates offered in the tables printed in their Sunday newspapers, everyone's happy. But as soon as the crunch comes, the 'investments' offered as collateral for this borrowing from the public are exposed for the dogs they are. And as soon as the influx of money from investors dries up, there's nothing left with which to honour the company's hollow promises.

In summary, we can reasonably lay the charge that since the financial deregulation of the early 1980s, we have witnessed over two decades of the most incompetent central banking the world has ever experienced. Central banks welcomed in deregulation — then they saw the evil it was doing and managed to comprehensively stuff up its administration. Former Federal Reserve chairmen Paul Volcker and Alan Greenspan have acknowledged this, as has Mervyn King of the

Bank of England, and they have made the appropriate expressions of mea culpa.

In New Zealand, I think our Reserve Bank governors have been far less impressive. Worse, all recent ones are on record whining about the excesses of the out-of-control housing market, deploring it as a grotesque misallocation of scarce investment resources, apparently seeing no irony in the fact that the situation has come about due in no small measure to the deterioration in prudential controls of the banks over which they have presided. Alan Bollard has even gone so far as to acknowledge that the current period has seen some of the greatest wealth destruction ever, yet he still fails to acknowledge that he and his predecessors' governance has been a large part of the problem.

Consequences for New Zealand of tighter global credit

As the world's banks — those that have survived — scramble to avoid insolvency, hoarding rather than lending out any cash they can get hold of, the pressure on economies grows immense. Businesses and households cannot function in a modern economy without access to credit, and so the reverberations of the crunch are substantial.

The central banks have moved in to relieve banks of their non-performing assets, to buy 'toxic' ones from them and to generally ensure the assets on banks' balance sheets are of sufficient quality to match the cash deposits and borrowings they maintain on their liabilities side. But such is the wildfire effect of the current economic meltdown that as fast as central banks can purge the duds from the banks' books, assets that were perfectly sound a matter of months ago are plunging in value to the point where they are worthless (toxic). This means that the massive effort to deleverage the world's banks has become open-ended. Central banks have come to resemble hamsters in a treadmill, and the long-delayed recession inevitably lingers.

Where does New Zealand sit in all this? We are a small trading nation that sells our goods and services around the world and spends the proceeds on the things we all like — notably electronic goods, travel and vehicles, none of which we produce onshore. We spend more on our imported luxuries than we earn for our exports, and the difference is termed our 'balance of payments deficit'. This is a debt that we must service by borrowing more from abroad each year or by selling assets to foreigners.

As you can see from the graph below, we run this deficit year after year, and since 2002, our position has steadily deteriorated:

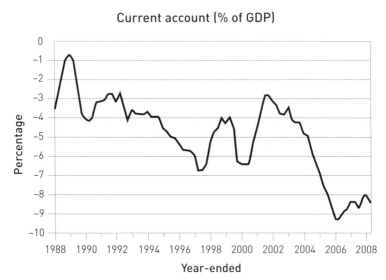

Current account (% of GDP)

Source: Statistics New Zealand

And the graph on the next page shows the consequence. Our level of indebtedness relative to our earnings has risen as we've been forced to borrow to pay for our expensive tastes in imported goods.

It's as though we've been using our credit card to pay off our overdraft. Our high level of indebtedness has made us quite vulnerable in this credit crunch environment, because if our creditors decide to charge us more on our borrowings, then our incomes will inevitably be squeezed. New Zealand is on 'credit watch' these days, which means that there's a possibility, if we continue to show little sign of getting our borrowings under control, that we will face higher bills to foreign creditors. Minister of Finance Bill English has cited this as one reason government can't spend our way out of trouble. We are near the end of our long and winding road of borrow, borrow, borrow.

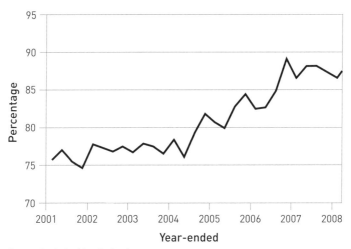

Net external debt (% of GDP)

Source: Statistics New Zealand

Central banks & financial deregulation — it came, they saw and it conquered them

We've seen that even though New Zealand didn't go in for the stupidity of lending money to poor folks in trailer parks who couldn't afford it, or for the naïve securitisation of such loans, we've been guilty of our own forms of fiscal folly. We've lately seen credit calamities with finance companies and an orgy of housing speculation fuelled by imprudent lending. With banks deciding that they no longer gave a toss about the quality of the asset-backing of their loans so long as their clients' cash flow looked healthy, we were headed for trouble. Sure enough, as soon as recession descended, our banks were as exposed as any others; it was inevitable that the taxpayer would eventually have to guarantee to depositors that their money was safe, because there was a real risk that confidence in the banking system would otherwise collapse. In the event, the government was forced to extend that guarantee — a last-resort measure — well before the over-exposure of our banks to foolish property loans had played out. This was because overseas confidence in banks had already ruptured, and several had even fallen over. As some lenders folded, those still standing blinked when asked to lend to other banks. Fear took root like wildfire; we were merely caught in the global blaze.

You can't blame the individual New Zealander for borrowing to excess, as for a while it made perfect sense — at least in the short term, until some party-pooper closed the whole show down. For a decade or more, there was easy money to be made from the capital gains on housing, as everybody was playing the same game. And should the highly geared face cash-flow problems, banks were only too happy to use 'modern financing techniques' to release equity, extending mortgages in line with house price appreciation.

Meanwhile, the world was being glutted with liquidity. The OPEC countries had loosened their purse strings, as had booming economies such as China. A virtuous cycle ensued — easier and easier borrowing conditions from the banks, the collapse of prudential discipline facilitated by reserve banks, frenzied investors driving the prices of land and housing up, encouraging banks to deploy still more credit to the residential, farming and commercial property sectors; it was just about impossible to borrow and lose.

Of course, everybody becomes a loser once the supply of credit dries up, which it now has. If poetic justice were at work, the only casualties would be the gamblers playing the property bubble who were caught with their debts maxed out just when the credit rug was pulled from under us all. But poetic justice is just another scarce commodity in this type of situation. The biggest loser is really the taxpayer, who has been called on to guarantee the funds of those who have supplied the wherewithal for this madness to occur — the depositors in our banks. As house prices now fall and distressed or mortgagee sales occur, any losses the lenders face are in effect underwritten by the rest of us. That's right, regardless of whether we had anything to do with this failure, it will be you and me who will pay the price for the excesses of the speculators and the prudential negligence of our Reserve Bank.

This isn't normal. Under 'normal' commercial terms, you would expect the banks to take the hit, their profits to fall and any losses to be made good first from shareholders' funds and, if necessary, this pain to reach out and hit depositors as banks are forced to declare they're in a position of insolvency. But the government has pre-empted this normal reward for commercial error by providing the depositor guarantee. Put simply, the international destructive mix of ineptitude (on the part of central banks), myopia (on the part of lending banks) and greed (on the part of borrowers) has resulted in a problem so large that the world's financial system is on the precipice. The global economy can't function without a banking system, so desperate remedies have been applied.

It's not as though any of this should have taken our Reserve Bank by surprise. After all, as noted above, New Zealand's orgy of borrow and spend has produced a humdinger in its external accounts, which now sees the country on credit watch. This is a curious thing, when you consider how healthy our export earnings have been. When in our history have we seen record prices for our commodities coinciding with a record deficit in our external accounts? That's quite a feat, even for the most spendthrift of economies. Have a look at the graph below.

Traditionally we have run into a balance of payments deficit when our economy has kept expanding at a time when commodity prices have slumped, but this time around we have managed — courtesy of the credit boom — to blow the deficit out in spite of a boom in our

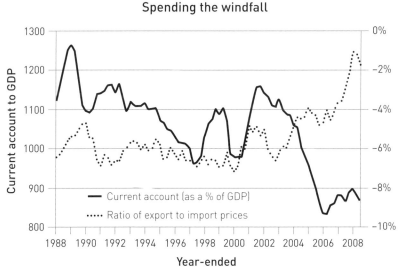

Spending the windfall

Source: Statistics New Zealand

overseas earnings. Nice work.

If ever there was a red light in the cockpit indicating that something was fundamentally out of whack in the New Zealand economy, this was it, and it's been a stall-warning indicator blazing in the vision of our regulators for several years now. Yet our policymakers did nothing, simply because the view of all that blue sky out the window was so mesmerising — successive years of economic growth must mean we're flying.

The crime of the policymakers was they didn't care that the growth we were enjoying was clearly unsustainable. They would be less blameworthy if they'd been unaware of the massive 'structural imbalances' that existed in the economy. Instead, however, 'structural imbalances' became a kind of catch-phrase in policy circles, a quip to describe 'condition normal', as it became patently obvious that the savers of the world were financing more and more spending by the borrowers of the world.

For a big borrowing economy like ours to swim against the tide of apparent wealth creation would have meant tightening credit by adjusting prudential ratios on banks, slowing our economy while the rest of the world was having a ball. But this would have required a long-term view. Such prescience from politicians or policy advisors, it is now painfully evident, is too much to expect. The lure of economic growth, no matter how temporary and how damaging to our long-term economic prospects, is all-consuming. The same nexus of mass greed and fear that drives speculative booms and busts also produces complacency and negligence on the part of policymakers, who find it impossible to focus on anything but the short term, for all the plethora of platitudes they mouth about the importance of the day after tomorrow.

In all, New Zealand has become one of the most exposed countries to the world's speculative bubble — it shows in house prices, it shows in farmland prices, and it shows in our external debt ratios, which stand among the highest in the world. Naïvely, the general view among New Zealand policymakers has been that because this debt is all private sector we need not be concerned; it's for the market to deal with. Well, that's just dandy — until the market *does* decide to deal with it, by tightening the supply of credit barbiturates that has fuelled our addiction and a gut-punched, general economic slump results. The real possibility of New Zealand suffering prolonged ramifications from the global credit crunch arises from our cavalier attitude to our external imbalance. We are so used to living beyond our means, thinking this is normal, that we still hear confident prognoses. You'll hear it said that because we don't have a subprime-mortgage sector, we won't face the same stress from the credit crunch as other countries.

As the graphs above indicate, such blasé complacency is little short of surreal, like denying the ship is sinking even as you tread water.

Sharing the pain

Who gets hurt in this retreat from the era of fast-and-loose credit?

▷ The borrowers are first in line — any equity they might have just vaporises as their creditors lay claim to their assets.

▷ Next, the supply of credit to those parts of the economy that aren't in trouble shrinks as the banks hoard cash. We're seeing it. Loans out to businesses — ultimately the only source of income growth for all New Zealanders — have dried up as banks scramble to hoard cash, and that of course pummels the real economy and, ultimately, jobs.

▷ This is a global crisis, so none of us are immune. We need to trade internationally to earn income, but the world isn't buying right now. Many firms are finding it a lot harder to sell their stuff, given the world is in recession. This creates local stress, and stressed firms look to cut costs and jobs.

In short, then, we all share the pain, and it's only once the squeeze eases internationally that we can start to say with confidence that our economy will stabilise and be in a position to resume growth. When even former Federal Reserve head Alan Greenspan is advocating the nationalisation of the banks — whereby US taxpayers become the new owners of some of these major institutions that have hit the wall — we know that the 2008 credit crunch has developed into a very serious international event indeed.

Globally, the rush to 'deleverage' — to reduce debt — is in full flight. Economists have a term for the unusual situation where a problem begun by endemic indebtedness is exacerbated by a general move to restore balance-sheet health and build up savings. Lord Keynes, arguably the greatest economist the world's ever seen, described this phenomenon as the 'paradox of thrift' — demand in the economy shrivels up as we all rush to raise our savings to a point where we feel safe from the ravages of recession.

If everyone suddenly tries to save rather than spends each dollar that comes our way, then the economy can end up in a hole — a hole of very low growth and high unemployment. And it can reach a kind of equilibrium — all the talk of the hole makes us fear for our own financial security, which means we save rather than spend — and unless something comes along to snap us out of it, we simply stay in that hole. The 1930s Depression was such an occurrence. That's why you hear our Reserve Bank governor, whose dire warnings about the poor savings record of New Zealanders are still ringing in our ears, urging us to spend, spend, spend for the economy's sake. Never mind if you personally go bust in the process, apparently — your country needs you!

This is why central banks and governments the world over have been loosening monetary policy and boosting government deficits in a desperate attempt to offset the impact of the private sector's U-turn from its late, lamented, big-spending ways. This policy response has worked in every recession we've seen since the 1980s, but it very much appears as though all those quick-fix solutions managed to achieve was to ramp up ever-higher private-sector debt ratios and deficits of income to spending against the day the Big One came along. The solutions in those cases have only contributed to the present problem. The graph on page 29 shows how this has worked in the New Zealand context.

So this is the current economic dilemma. Here in little old New Zealand, a cork that is bouncing around on the turbulent ocean of the

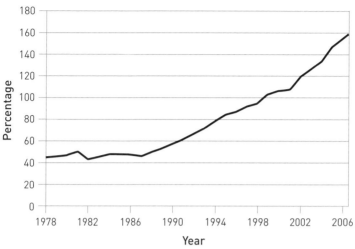

Household liabilities
(as % of disposable income)

Source: Statistics New Zealand

world economy, we are totally reliant on the governments of the world to successfully stimulate their economies, to restore the demand for goods and services from the private sector that has all but dried up. We can't take it for granted that their present efforts will work at all, let alone any time soon. The very best we can hope for is a grindingly slow climb out of the current slump — in other words, any prospective economic recovery will be anaemic.

Still, from our present position, any economic recovery, no matter how anaemic, would be most welcome. Let's have a look at how it might materialise.

2

Economic recovery without so much borrowing — really?

The mechanics of economic recovery

We'll know we have a full-scale economic recovery on our hands when everyone is buying and selling again, companies are taking on staff, banks are lending money, farmers are complaining about the high dollar and the Reserve Bank is warning us that inflation is nudging the upper limits of the target range. Remember those days?

So what has to change in the world situation for these things to come about?

At its very simplest, as a recession sets in, there's usually an apparent logical inconsistency: there are people wanting to buy more stuff and other people capable of producing it looking for work. So what's stopping them making beautiful music together?

Well, first off, wanting to buy more stuff is different from having the means to do it. In recent times, shopaholics in the developed world have had recourse to debt, and we Kiwis have certainly been among the front ranks of those who buy stuff using other people's money. Meanwhile, of course, we've been servicing those loans. The supply of new loans has dried up — that's what the 'credit crunch' is all about — and as unemployment rises, the debt-servicing obligations of those folk unlucky enough to find themselves out of work pretty quickly exhausts their discretionary income. They certainly can't keep on buying. On the other hand, producers — both here and overseas — stand ready to produce as much as is needed. They aren't going to produce in the hope they can find buyers, though; in a climate of fear, they definitely want to see the colour of our money first.

This retrenching of spending and replenishing of savings drives the economy into the ground. It's a self-feeding pattern — as producers cut back on production they need fewer workers and that of course means less income into households, still less spending, even less production required, and so on. A downward spiral of economic activity ensues once the credit crunch frightens us all to keep our wallets in our pockets. What might break the cycle?

Conventionally, as demand falls away, the prices for goods and services are cut in response — at least to the point where producers can no longer make any profit, but seldom below that level. In turn, pressure goes on the prices of inputs into the production process — commodity prices, labour and other manufactured imports. Needless to say, if there's pressure on wages, such that there are nil wage rises or even net falls in wage levels, the amount of discretionary cash out there to create demand for consumer goods declines further, putting yet more pressure on prices, and so on.

And exacerbating this 'deflationary spiral' is the effect it has on the expectations of people who *are* in the position to buy stuff. If you expect prices tomorrow to be cheaper than they are today, then why buy today what you can put off until tomorrow anyway? And if we all behave like that, our deflationary economic contraction could plunge even deeper.

The circuit breaker! Where's the circuit breaker? Conventionally, it lies within the financial system, where we would see a fall in the price of credit — that is, interest rates, which in New Zealand are influenced by the Reserve Bank's 'official cash rate' — as economic activity contracts, the demand for borrowing plunges and the supply of savings soars. At some point, the cost of borrowing money becomes so cheap that the risk-takers among us — and without risk-takers, we're all doomed — decide that they *will* take a chance, they will borrow and invest. Greed will overpower fear and save us all.

The decision by risk-takers to take the plunge again is a stimulus to economic activity in itself, as the investment process requires people to be hired, materials to be purchased and industrial production and services to be expanded. If the risk-taking, entrepreneurial sector gets its expectations right, can produce products that people want at the prices they can afford, and can excite demand sufficiently so that they buy today rather than putting it off until tomorrow, then we have an economic recovery on our hands. Yeeeehaaaaa!

But it seems like a hell of a lot of ducks to get in a row first, doesn't it? After all, the very greed that may yet save us got us into this mess in the first place, didn't it? How are the risk-takers who lately crashed and burned, taking their creditors with them, going to persuade those creditors to trust them, that this time they know what they're doing? Certainly, the higher the cliff from which the economy is falling, the more you're asking of the risk-taking, entrepreneurial sector and its financiers to dig us all out by carrying on as though it were business-as-usual in the face of a spending contraction all around.

This is why it's a worry that, left to its own devices, the private economy may in fact not stabilise and turn around until unemployment rises and misery sinks to socially disturbing levels, threatening the whole socio-political fabric. It's a race to see who wins between the forces of doom and gloom tearing the economy apart, and the animal spirits of the gung-ho, well-heeled risk-takers recovering their gumption, spurred on perhaps by the prospect of zero returns from safe-haven bank deposits. When does investor fear turn into investor appetite for return? How long do they need to endure zero returns (or worse) from safe investments before they get itchy financial feet?

Answer: we don't know!

Typically, government and their policy advisors are impatient to find out, too. So they get all too readily gripped by the need to 'do something'. By contrast with the policy lethargy that prevails during an economic boom, a slump galvanises policy flurries, some of which work, many of which don't.

So in wades the government — as agent for the population overall. The government has a monopoly power to levy taxes, although it may, in the interim, borrow from its own central bank to create ready money, against the day when taxes have to be raised or the decision is made to borrow from the public. Either way, the government can begin spending now and try, all by itself, to precipitate an economic turnaround. It's for recommending this course of action that Lord Keynes is reckoned to have made a major contribution to economic wisdom, as it's this tactic that is attributed with having brought to an end the period of debt-induced, downward spiralling that was the Great Depression.

This is why, across the world right now, we're seeing almost all governments signing up to what gets called 'quantitative easing' and 'expansionary fiscal policies'. What this means in English is that central banks are being directed to purchase dodgy assets and long-term government bonds from the banks and the public, so that the holders end up with (spendable) cash in their hands. At the same time, governments are outlining plans for all manner of spend-ups on cycle tracks and other forms of infrastructure, plus tax cuts (despite the very real fear that we'll all just save the latter) so that the full arsenal of the government sector is lined up against the forces of recession that threaten to tip into depression.

Will it work? Probably, but at the end of the day, we can also expect taxpayers to face a marked rise in taxes down the track to pay for it all. That day can be delayed until the economy from which governments generate their incomes is in a healthier state. So the process appears to be for the government to take off our hands all the bad debts we've been lumbered with, for government debt to subsequently rise to the heavens and then, after we're all back spending again, for inflation to be unleashed so that the real value of debts, including any the government takes on to help us out, just melts away.

From a wealth-preserving perspective then, you have to:

▷ get your debt down so you don't get done in by your creditors, bankrupted and lose all your assets;

▷ live well within your means so that if and when you lose your job, you can last on savings until things improve;

▷ be aware that once the recovery is embedded, it is likely that governments will allow inflation to flourish, so petrified of slipping back into recession will they be. This will be the time to buy property again. If you buy it too soon, you could well be part of the meltdown rather than the recovery.

Back to the macroeconomics. What if the government spending plan only works partially, stopping the worst of the rot, but only managing to deliver a low-growth, high-unemployment result? Can the government just keep spending willy-nilly forever?

No. This is where the quality of the government's spend is critical — the less effective its spend is in terms of raising the economy's productivity and international competitiveness, the more likely its efforts will simply contribute to an ever-burgeoning balance of payments deficit — and remember, we are starting this whole process with that deficit already blown out. Blow it too much more and we'll get caught in a vortex of a plunging currency and the soaring cost of servicing external debt — very Latin American indeed.

Any proposed government spending has to have a lasting, positive impact on the economy and living standards if we're to escape that fate, so it isn't just a licence to spend on anything that shows a sign of moving. Though having said that, it would be too hopeful to think that governments won't spend on wasteful endeavours — the pressure from sector lobbies moving in on politicians who are playing Santa will see to that, as will the desperation of our politicians as they eye their re-election prospects in the face of an economy that seems to be taking forever to get up. So spend big, spend fast may well win the day. Hang on to your hat.

What if we end up in a scenario where the government, through low-quality spending, actually exhausts its capacity to precipitate another economic recovery — like lighting your last match on a pile of wet wood? In this situation, we would see demand in the economy rekindled courtesy of the government spend, but that demand ending up being self-limiting through the exacerbation of those two, well-known imbalances that always restrict how fast the New Zealand economy can grow — inflation and/or the balance of payments deficit. A credit downgrade in the midst of a government spend-up would inflict savage penalties on the New Zealand economy.

In conclusion, the international reaction to the asset bubble — namely the onset of the credit crunch — has set in train a global recession. New Zealand, despite the denials of the most leveraged in our economy, has little choice but to be swept along by those forces, and we are already suffering falls in income as the economy contracts. The government will (as it must) attempt to limit the depth of the recession, but its prospects of success are at the mercy of how much further the international pressures of contraction have to travel, plus the quality of the government's own spend — whether it boosts or deteriorates the productivity and international competitiveness of our productive sector.

The prospect of a low-growth, high-unemployment outcome cannot be dismissed — merely because the world economy has generated such huge imbalances on the road to this asset bubble. Correcting these imbalances could be well nigh impossible to accomplish without world growth dropping a wheel into some serious potholes; yet corrected they must be, because they lie at the heart of the global recession as surely as they lay at the heart of the boom. We're talking here about the major imbalances between countries that run a surplus and countries that run a deficit — those that earn more than they spend, and those that spend more than they earn. These imbalances have grown so large over the last decade that, in short, economic growth in debt-laden, spendthrift economies such as ours is no longer possible without recourse to other people's money.

Let's look at these imbalances more closely.

Global imbalances — why they must go if world growth is to resume

As the graph on page 36 illustrates, the imbalances have become huge compared to historical norms, and this is the major reason why global coupling remains so strong and it's near-impossible for some of the

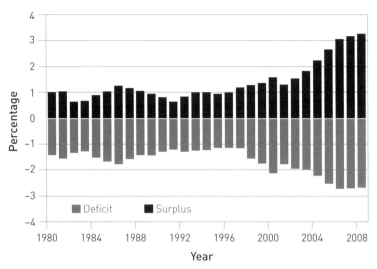

The imbalances — World Current Account
(% of GDP)

Source: International Monetary Fund, World Economic Outlook Database October 2008

major economies in the world to keep growing while others remain mired in recession — it's all or nothing nowadays, it seems.

The morbid dependency that has developed sees the OPEC and industrialising, emerging economies lending their surpluses to the profligate, mature economies that have become addicted to debt. And yet the two groups need each other — without the big-spending of the spendthrift consumers, manufacturers and the producers of commodities don't have a market. So they lend the consumers in countries such as the US, Australia and New Zealand the funds that enable them to carry on their spendthrift way. It seems absurd that China, say, would lend others the funds to enable those countries to pay for goods they buy from China. But that's what the global imbalances indicate is happening.

It seems the profligate consumer will just keep on spending until his creditor pulls the rug out, and this has now happened. But it's not just a problem for the profligate consumer. The butterfly flapped its wings in the consumer markets in the US, and a tornado of destruction ripped through the production sectors of China, the oil-producing countries and all the rest of us to boot. So just a slight hesitation of the borrow-and-spend trend from consumers and the world economy has ground to a standstill — so interwoven are the lines of dependency across the world between creditor and debtor, consumer and producer.

The notion, then, that governments can turn their economies around by stepping in and borrowing and spending where the private sector has stopped, is a little far-fetched, given that the global imbalance between debtor and creditor is so great that a single hesitation has put the world economy on ice. No, the fiscal spend-up may be a necessary condition to stopping the recessionary slide, but it looks like too much of a forlorn hope now to expect that it would be enough to get the wheels of commerce spinning in any sustainable fashion. Neither is the inevitable outcome of the banking sector collapse — wherein governments have to take over major banks and, in their desperation to see economic growth resume, order those banks to 'lend again' — likely to be a sufficient initiative to deliver us into a brave new world of economic growth and sustained rises in living standards. No. What has to happen is, quite simply, that the size of the imbalances, and the degree to which the surplus countries depend on deficit ones, have to reduce.

How might this come about? If the government spend-ups can slow the pace of the slide in confidence — and the decline in economic activity that's accompanying the reduction of debt by those households, businesses and countries that have become addicted — then there's a good chance lenders will willingly shoulder risk again, pop up out of their toxic-loan-induced foxholes and resume their financing of risk-takers. But it goes without saying that the borrowers have to have stronger balance sheets so that their chances of default are much reduced. Yes, they have to increase savings to do that — back to the paradox of thrift.

It is no good relying on inflation to erode away all the debt burdens and kick-start recovery. The inflation outbreak is very much the secondary phase of a recovery process, not the primary. It must be preceded by a real recovery, wherein government spending, or private investment, or both act to turn the juggernaut around. And the private sector will need not just very poor returns from safe-haven investments to encourage it to set sail, but also decent returns on offer from the investment opportunities that remain. Which brings us finally to rates of return.

The return of reward for risk

It seems inescapable that for a global recovery to have any substance, we have to see the rates of return on loans and investments restored to magnitudes that reflect an adequate margin over and above the risk-free rate — that is, the rate that the government offers on its debt, over and above inflation, and neutral of tax. How else are the risk-takers going to summon the courage to take a punt again? To rely on capital gains to compensate for the lack of a competitive cash return is a far-fetched notion in a world where asset prices are under pressure from the profligate being forced to save and then invest rather than to borrow and invest. Hence investors will require adequate cash compensation — a return to the good old days, before many of today's participants in the economy were out of school.

Where does this leave us? A rise in running yields the ratio of the annual income generated by an asset to the price of that asset on assets across the board looks a certainty. And in an economy that is slowing, there's little likelihood that this will come about through a rise in earnings. More likely it will be falls in asset prices that will play their part in realigning this number (earnings yield) with the yield available from the competing, risk-free rate that government paper offers.

Footnote — systemic disease in our financial sector

All of the above makes good sense from an economist's perspective of where we are, how we got here, how we can get out, and what's more likely to occur. There's just one last factor to address — we have a systemic disease running riot in our financial services sector that, unless it is dealt with, will forever doom New Zealand to be a poor-quality investment, and a low-growth, low-income society.

The behavioural swine flu that is running amok in our financial service businesses takes the form of a total dereliction of care to the very savers that provide its lifeblood: the funding. We've seen it in the raft of poor-quality lending; in the misrepresentation of high-risk investment opportunities as low-risk, conservative options; in the absence of accountability for those misleading the public; and in the utter ineffectiveness of the regulatory framework that has allowed the cowboys and shysters that populate the ranks of finance companies, financial advisory firms and even the banks to wreak the havoc that they have. Without a lift of standards, the saving public will rightfully continue to distrust this industry and we will fail to attain an economically efficient allocation of our scarce capital resources — essential if living standards are to be raised.

Much of the rest of this book is devoted to outlining what's so wrong — morally and ethically — with this sector, how it has to be cleaned up and what investors should do in the meantime.

3

Reality check: Who needs economic growth anyway?

I rode a camel; my son drives a Mercedes; his son pilots a Lear jet; his son will ride a camel.

Sheik Rashid of Dubai

The treadmill of economic growth — can't I just get off?

With all this talk of investment doom and gloom, it's easy to forget to take the long view. And taking the long view, we have all been getting richer and richer. Interestingly, just as this crash comes along, increasing numbers of people seem to be asking: 'Why bother? It's such a drag having to work all the time anyway. Why do we need economic growth at all? Haven't most of us got enough?'

This is a fair question, and a particularly salient one for citizens of the world's richer societies to be asking. It has probably crossed the minds of each of us at some stage — particularly in those moments where we start to feel like a hamster running on a wheel, working our little butts off — for what? Just to pay for the latest gadget demanded by our teenage offspring? So why can't we just say no to the Xboxes, the iPhones, the USB rocket launchers, and forsake economic growth?

And why does the government in particular seem so obsessed with keeping the wheels of growth turning — even when the hamsters turning the wheels are you and me, voters who would rather just kick back in our burrows (or on the beach)? Surely, some day, the hamsters of the world should unite and decide we've got enough cheese (what do hamsters eat anyway?), agree to get off the wheel, and go play in the sawdust together?

The irony of this question being asked by jaded Kiwis is that New Zealand has had the second-worst growth record in the OECD since 1970. Only Switzerland comes in worse.[1] Come to think of it, they beat us in the last America's Cup. Perhaps poor economic growth and sailing prowess are somehow correlated. It is, after all, a leisure pursuit for most. Maybe we should take those 'I'd rather be sailing' bumper stickers even more seriously.

We've been performing a bit better in recent times (since 2001), as the chart on the next page shows (and significantly or not, since we lost the America's Cup), but there are plenty of high-income countries that continue to make a far better fist of lifting the incomes of each of their citizens — Finland and Australia, for example. Scratching their heads over this poor performance record, our governments have made a mantra of growling at New Zealanders for our lack of a savings ethic, rapping our knuckles over our obsession with buying houses, and smacking the bottoms of Kiwi entrepreneurs for their tendency to stop growing their business as soon as they can afford their house, car and boat.

Growth in GDP per person over time

Throughout her time in office, Helen Clark was adamant that New Zealand should shortly come in the 'top half of the OECD' on indicators such as growth. This was unfortunate — we were overtaken by Greece and Slovenia (come on, Slovenia?) on her watch. John Key has announced an even more ambitious target: rather than simply getting in the top half, he's set his sights on matching our 12th-ranked neighbour, Australia. He's hazy on the details of how we are to achieve this, unless

GDP growth of selected countries

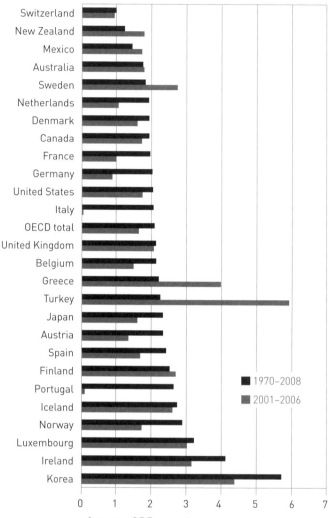

Average GDP growth rate per person per year

1970–2008
2001–2006

Source: OECD

he expects his tax cuts package to do it — or perhaps even the cycle track! — although New Zealanders will predictably devote their tax cuts to buying bigger houses and more boats. While we've kept up with Australia's growth rate since 2000, the damage was done in the previous three decades, when the income gap first emerged (see the chart above). We now need to grow faster than Australia merely to maintain the same absolute gap in income. The picture below is a bit like the runs required in one-day cricket — the further we fall behind the Aussie run-rate, the harder we'll have to hit the ball in the latter stages of the innings to catch up. The gap is already so big we'll need to bring back Lance Cairns and his Excalibur — we need to hit plenty of sixes.

The economic Chappell-Hadlee trophy — income per person

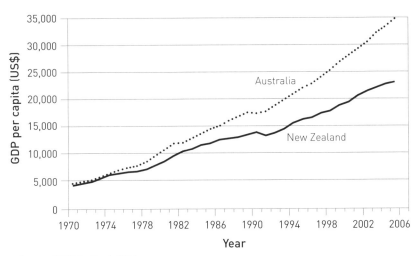

Source: *OECD Factbook 2008*

Maybe all this talk of giving up on growth is really just us Kiwis saying we aren't very good at this game so we'll take our bat and go home. Let's look at what no growth really means.

There's more to life . . . than GDP

GDP stands for gross domestic product, but that probably doesn't help you much. Simply put, it's the total value of all the stuff made in a country each year. We only count the value that is *added* within the country, so if we make a lawnmower here but have to buy in the steel from Australia, we'd count the value of the lawnmower *minus* the value of the steel. The value of the stuff made is determined by the price it is sold for, which is nice and easy to measure. The money from a sale has to go somewhere, so another way to look at GDP is the total of all the money (wages, salaries and profits) made from the country's working activity. In other words, it is the total of our income as a nation.

You might see one of the flaws straight away: *the value is the price paid.* Lots of things get bought that we don't really value — we buy some things because we have to; anyone who has been to a lawyer recently can attest to that. But GDP counts it. Building a new prison, or cleaning up rubbish after the Wellington Sevens Weekend all involves paying people for their work, so it's totted up on GDP. Similarly, finding a new gas field and selling the gas adds to GDP — although some may argue the extraction of resources and resulting carbon emissions incurs a cost to the planet that is not contemplated in the GDP reckoning. Simply totting up our incomes is by no means a comprehensive way to measure economic activity.

The really interesting question is what *isn't* included in GDP. GDP is supposed to be the value of all the goods and services created. But it only includes *marketed goods and services.* In other words, it doesn't include *illegal* transactions, or any situation where money doesn't change hands or isn't recorded (by the tax system, say). So if you pay the plumber in cash, that transaction doesn't appear in GDP. Similarly, if you do a DIY jobby on the plumbing, the value won't appear in GDP figures, either. But it should, because doing that plumbing job makes your life better (assuming you're not a walking DIY disaster zone).

Probably the biggest omission here in GDP figures is the value of unpaid work around the home. Cooking, being a strong, positive role model to the kids, growing veges — it's all unpaid, but by the same token it all certainly make us better off. It also saves households a lot of money — for example, in restaurant, grocery or babysitting bills. In 1999, Statistics New Zealand did a study and estimated the value of all this work was about 40 per cent of GDP.[2] But this is not added on to GDP because it is very expensive to repeat such a survey every year, and it would make it impossible to compare our GDP with overseas figures. Others don't care how the house husband spends his time while they're out doing real, paid work, so why should we?

In fact, our government already makes one big adjustment of GDP figures in order to make our figures more comparable with overseas. Different countries have very different rates of home ownership. If you rent a house, you pay your landlord and this will show up in GDP figures. But if you own a house, *you* are both landlord and renter — no money changes hands. This would make the GDP of countries with high rates of home ownership look poor, as they have less money changing hands. As a result, all countries adjust their GDP to take account of home-ownership rates. However, no adjustment takes place for the amount of veges you grow in your garden — or, for that matter, the number of deer you shoot or the amount of fish you catch and eat yourself. It's just too hard to make this adjustment, although the image of bespectacled statisticians visiting your home to count your tomato plants and estimate their yield is quite amusing.

So if you've ever been to Samoa and thought, 'I don't feel 12 times richer than these people,'[3] it's probably because you aren't, really. They probably grow or catch a lot of their own food, or even build their own houses. Maybe they even swap skills, and exchange through barter (you fix my roof and I'll give you a chook and three breadfruit) instead of using money. There's no doubt you're better off from such trading, but under the present rules, because no money changes hands, it's beneath the radar of measured GDP.

So what do people really mean when they talk about 'zero growth'? Do we want our aggregate income to stay exactly the same forever? Presumably, everyone wants their income to keep up with cost of living increases, otherwise you'd have a fixed income while prices rise, and you'd be progressively worse off. So we need to ward off the impact of the corrosive effect of inflation, which eats away at the value of our income through price rises. Once we take out inflation, we're talking about zero *real* GDP growth. Similarly, we probably want to remove the impact of population changes. If the national income pie stays the same size, every time a new worker is grown or an immigrant arrives from abroad and sits down to dinner, we'll all have to take a smaller slice. So we're really talking about zero real GDP growth per person, otherwise known as *'per capita'*.

To see what a big difference population growth can make, have a look at the chart below. Almost half of our GDP growth since 1960 can be accounted for by population increase.

Difference between GDP growth and GDP per person

Source: *Earth Trends* 4

Overall, the graph above shows GDP per person is about 10 times what it was in 1960. I can hear the hippy in all of us crying already: 'Hey, man. Like, no *way* is life in New Zealand ten times better than it was in the sixties.' Now here's the rub: GDP figures were never designed to value our *quality* of life; they were created to tally up how much stuff we make and sell. Not everything that made you happy in the '60s ended up in GDP figures: strumming a guitar, singing Kumbaya around the fireside, making daisy chains — alas, not even LSD-fuelled love-ins cut it with this measure of value-add.

Back to the point. We need some growth in incomes (or production sold) to counteract inflation (the higher cost of goods and services) and population growth, otherwise our personal buying power will fall over time. So those of us yearning to step down from the production treadmill are really talking about having zero growth in real GDP per person, not bringing the economy (as we measure it) to a standstill.

Now that we can agree on what we mean by ending the pursuit

of economic growth, let's look at what it would mean for us as a country and for you and me as individuals.

See you Sunday, Willie

There are three basic ways that you can lift your income, and the same logic applies to the country as a whole. You can either work *harder* or work *smarter* or *use more machines* (although in practice, using more or better machines is often part of working smarter). Working harder could mean putting more time in on the job (maybe working overtime, or taking fewer holidays; how many of us have a dedicated workmate — Willie — who regularly works Sundays in order to keep his place on the treadmill?). Working smarter is about earning more for the same level of effort, perhaps by increasing the efficiency of the means by which your effort is converted to remuneration. Using more machines is pretty self-explanatory: it's increasing the amount of non-people resources we use. As an example, in the bad old days when people wore walk shorts, sandals and long socks to work, offices used to have typing pools. To get something typed, you had to write it out by hand, and then get someone to type it (usually accompanied with a bribe to get it done on time). Nowadays, we use more machines by having a computer on our own desk, and this incidentally allows us to work smarter by typing for ourselves — although all those two-finger, 'hunt and peck' typists out there are probably acutely nostalgic for the typing pool.

When people object to economic growth it is usually because they equate it with either working harder or using more natural resources (i.e. machines). But presumably you wouldn't turn down an opportunity to work smarter. The only problem is that New Zealand doesn't have a great record of working smarter compared to overseas, as the chart on page 48 shows. Since 1990 only about a quarter of New Zealand's real GDP growth has come from working smarter,[5] while most has come from working harder. On the national scale, working harder generally means higher employment rather than everyone being Willie on a

Sunday and working longer hours. Finland has worked *less* hard since 1985 and yet it still grew faster than us — because those canny Finns worked a lot smarter (mostly by being smart enough to have Nokia).

Working smarter vs working harder vs using more machines 1985–2006

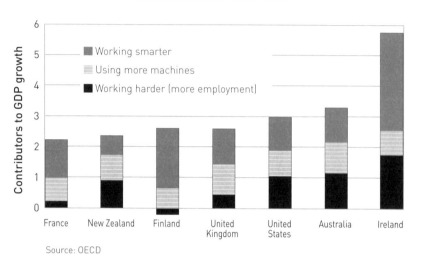

Source: OECD

So we've proven that we can still have a little bit of GDP growth (0.63 per cent per annum) without anyone working harder or using more machines. But as the graph shows, we're not that smart at working smarter. There are limits to how much harder you can work or how many machines we can build with increasingly limited natural resources (unless we start mining asteroids), so why can't we work as smartly as those other countries? Given our atrocious record in this regard, it probably makes sense for us as a country to focus less on working harder and using more machines, and more on trying to work smarter. Who knows? If we get smarter, we might even engineer a rise in the price we get for what we make. Wouldn't that be cool — working smarter, half as many hours, no more machines to baffle us with their improved user-interface and six-volume *Getting Started User Guide*, and still doubling our income — all because we make stuff for which the world is prepared to pay more.

If we still decide we want zero growth in our per capita incomes and we can count on the pathetic little bit we squeeze from using our 'smarts' (that paltry 0.63 per cent of income growth), this gives us some choices. We could work smarter and work fewer hours — that is, reduce weekly working hours as we reap the rewards of working smarter and growing our income, or retire earlier. Or we could use fewer machines per person, and reduce the strain we are putting on the planet's limited resources.

Don't worry, be wealthy

Governments and economists alike have for years been startled that all this wealth we have doesn't seem to make us any happier. As a result, they've started looking at the links between happiness (or 'satisfaction', or 'well-being') and GDP. This has unleashed a tidal wave of academic papers and has governments around the world all in a tizz questioning whether they should switch to targets of well-being rather than economic growth. God help us if the government thinks it can make us happier! I wonder who the Minister for Happiness will be — bring back Nandor Tanczos?

There *is* a link between income and happiness, but the link isn't very strong. Generally each country has the same pattern — richer people are happier than poor people. Looking across countries, increases in happiness taper off pretty quickly after around US$10,000–12,000 of income per person per year. The average income for New Zealand is already about double this, so we're into the misery zone. This same result holds true within a country over time — poor countries get happier as their income rises, but rich countries generally haven't been getting happier as they've got richer still.

So if money can't buy happiness, what can? The simplest response is that no one really knows. The answer is buried under a huge number of possible variables, all of which overlap and affect each other. National factors such as democracy, human rights, the level of corruption, and political and social stability may all have an impact. On a more personal level, health, relationships, membership of voluntary organisations, a sense of purpose and meaning, and optimism and trust have a strong role to play also.[6]

Ultimately, then, happiness levels are a pretty personal thing. Maybe our happiness level is even built-in — some studies have shown that people who were happier in their twenties go on to earn more later in their lives. This, of course, makes the job difficult for people who try to replace GDP with another measure — it's pretty hard to nail down a measure that captures everything that might be important to different people. To simplify things in creating their Human Development Index, the United Nations whittled it down to four factors — life expectancy, literacy, education participation, and income.[7] The only other method is to ask people directly how happy or satisfied they are — but quite apart from the fact that the answer will vary depending on what sort of day they're having, the aggregated answers won't tell anyone how to improve general happiness.

The final piece of the puzzle is that, actually, income *does* influence our happiness, but not in the way you might think. After the US$10,000 point is reached, *relative* wealth is more important for happiness than *absolute* wealth. As a result, we get some funny paradoxes — the richest people in America are about as happy as the Maasai tribe in Africa. The Maasai do pretty well as far as Africans go — they are successful cattle farmers — but they have no electricity. Conversely, slum dwellers

Life satisfaction rating for selected groups

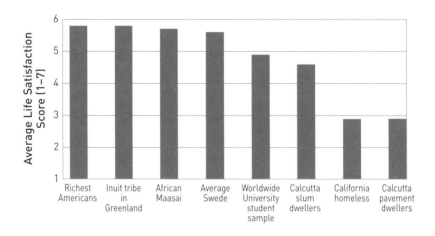

Source: Diener and Seligman, *Beyond Money*

in Calcutta are far happier than the homeless in California, although the homeless in California generally have a higher income.

Perhaps more importantly, although happiness doesn't rise with income, happiness *falls* when income falls.[8] So while we might be a bit jaundiced about the prospect of getting richer, no one wants to get any poorer.

So why don't we all chuck in the day job and get ourselves a nice plot of land to live the 'good life'? Most of us have the choice, but generally speaking, we don't do it — at least, not much. The graph below compares the hours worked per year by the average worker in New Zealand with our counterparts in Australia, the US, France, the EU 15 (basically Western Europe) and the OECD as a whole. Working hours for us, the Aussies, the Yanks and across the OECD have dropped a little bit, but have generally been quite steady. However, in Europe and France in particular, working hours have been falling more rapidly.

Another way to enjoy the fruits of rising incomes is to retire early. Surprisingly, the trends across countries for early retirement are

Hours worked per person per year — international comparisons

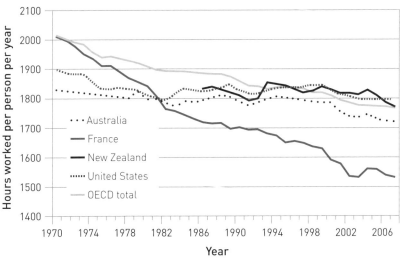

Source: *OECD Factbook 2009*

similar to those with shorter working hours — Europe has had the largest increase in early retirement rates while those in the English-speaking world have been slowly declining or have stayed the same.[9]

French happiness levels seem to have been increasing over the time that their hours have dropped (although they are yet to match happiness levels in New Zealand — maybe us being last in the 'smarts' stakes, as we discussed above, makes us really happy!).[10] Ignorance really is bliss!

Life satisfaction levels by country (2006)

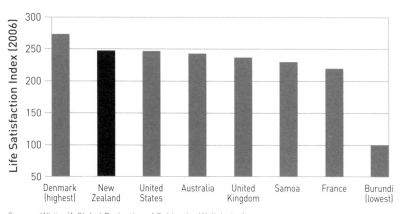

Source: White, 'A Global Projection of Subjective Well-being'

So why don't we kick back with a glass of wine and enjoy life a little like the French do? The answer is buried in the happiness examples above. Extra income makes us happy up to a certain point — presumably enough to meet our basic needs of food, warmth and shelter. Beyond that, extra income generally only makes us happier if it increases our *status* by making us better off than the Joneses next door. The question is, who do you compare yourself to? The people next door? The rest of the country? Or Australians? The answer could matter a lot for your desired income, your happiness levels, and for whether you want to step off the hamster wheel and nibble the cheese for a while. John Key obviously thinks the Aussies matter, as do the thousands of Kiwis who shift there every year.

How do the French and the Europeans get over this problem of pay-cheque envy? Simple: they take away the opportunity for people to work harder. Part of the reason for the recent big drop in French working hours is probably the institution of the compulsory 35-hour working week. Most governments in Europe also tend to operate heavily regulated labour markets. This means it's very difficult to get a job, but once you have one, it's very hard to lose it. This is great for those who have a job, but it's not so great for those who can't get a job at all. This seems to be one of the major reasons behind the recent riots in France, as unemployed, bored youngsters hit back against the system that denies them a chance to get started in life. Some researchers argue that money is the least important aspect of working — it is the associated success and achievement that really impacts on our happiness.[11] So there is a flaw in the European system — sometimes people want to work hard. And thank goodness for that, otherwise nothing would get done.

However, it's food for thought, isn't it? If our government legislates for shorter working hours, we could end up poorer but happier — apart from those who can't get a job.

Money makes the hamster wheel go round

A major reason for the growth obsession, as discussed above, is envy. Maybe we are kept on the hamster wheel simply because that is what the people next door are doing. This doesn't seem like a great reason, but how can it be stopped? Should we all agree to hop off the hamster wheel at the same time, or just get over our envy? And even if our whole country agreed to stop growing and have more time fishing, how would we feel every time we watched US sitcoms and Aussie soaps? Would the envy return — and our levels of life satisfaction plummet — when we saw the new household cleaning robot on *Neighbours?*

And don't forget government. For every extra dollar earned by the country, the government snaffles just under 40 per cent through various taxes. So a more cynical reason for governments to want GDP growth is that it gives them more of our money to spend without their having to raise tax rates — which is a pretty unpopular, and therefore a politically risky thing to do. If we were content as a nation to curb economic growth, would we also be happy for the government to freeze spending increases on health and education? Probably not. After all, the Satisfaction Index suggests that the top three keys to improving life satisfaction are (in order of importance) health, education and income.[12] The first two are chiefly a result of government spending (which grows as GDP grows), and the last is GDP itself.

Now then, let's consider a few really good reasons for wanting economic growth.

▷ **Does more money make us better people?** Some researchers claim that increasing wealth actually improves society and perhaps even makes us better people.[13] Economic growth is linked with democracy and tolerance (for instance, of minorities). However, it's difficult to know which is the chicken and which is the egg, so to speak. One theory is that growth allows an increase in spare time, allowing the population of richer countries to put more time into all the good causes that go with champagne socialism. So when times are good we are more likely to be good citizens, respect the rights of others, and care more for animals and the environment. Conversely, when times are bad, there is a tendency towards increased violence and xenophobia, and you might get so desperate you start to view the family pet as a possible roast dinner. Some researchers believe a permanent era of zero growth could turn us all into militant rednecks, happy living in our caravan so long as we had a bottle of whiskey, plenty of shotgun shells and someone else to blame for all our problems.

▷ **Big Brother's hand-me-downs.** If our GDP falls further behind the rest of the world, it's unlikely we'll be able to afford the latest technology — at least not as quickly as we can now. If the thought of fewer people talking on their cellphone loudly on the bus pleases you, just have a think about what that means for your sons and daughters. If we live off the technology hand-me-downs of other countries, our children are much less likely to become the next Bill Gates. Our 'inventions' will be 20 years behind. Think of India, still making Royal Enfields and Morris Oxfords.

▷ **Gazump: I'll see your bid, and raise you.** As the saying goes, they aren't making any more land. There's some truth to this, although not so true as it was reckoned to be during the recent property boom. But if the incomes of New Zealanders froze while the United States continued to grow, over time the Yanks would increasingly be able to outbid New Zealanders for limited resources — a chunk of Coromandel beachfront, for example, or a resort in Fiji. Where there is bidding for a limited supply of a certain commodity, whether it be gold Rolexes or barrels of oil, the wealthier person will win.

▷ **Please sir, can I have some more?** Ask any union — people never like getting paid less. Industries and businesses will always rise and fall, but while the economy is growing, wages in poorly performing businesses don't usually fall, they just rise more slowly than others. Over time, people spot the difference and move. With zero growth, however, the adjustment would be starker. People in poorly performing businesses would generally have to take a pay cut, and probably wouldn't take kindly to that.

▷ **A rising tide.** Finally, and probably the best reason for growth, is that it is good for the poor. It is all very well for the middle and upper classes to push away their plates and belch when they've had their fill of economic growth. They were lucky enough to attend the banquet. The poor, by contrast, have been picking up the crumbs from under the table. If they decide they haven't quite had their fill yet, then economic growth is the surest way to raise their living standards.[14] This is the problem with the French approach — while it takes away the pressure on the middle and upper classes to keep up with the Joneses, it also holds back the very poor and often prevents them from working at all.

Yes, yes, it's a treadmill — but the most important thing, and a thing we can easily overlook when we are so focused on trying to run faster on our hamster wheel, is that each of us has the choice of whether to stay on the hamster wheel or not. If you feel you have enough, step off and spend some quality hamster time. The point is that we each have the choice to step off. It's just in the national psyche to keep the wheel spinning.

A deliberate policy choice to restrict growth as a nation would be the worst present we have accepted from the French since we gave Alain Mafart and Dominique Prieur visitor visas. This decision would probably hurt the worst-off in society, as they are the ones who stand to gain the most from further growth. It would also rob motivated people of the opportunity to work hard and follow their dreams. Hopefully we don't need to go as far as France and much of Western Europe in using regulation to restrict our freedom to choose which particular facet of quality of life we prefer, as this could have long-term, negative consequences. But so long as we leave people with the choice to pursue a higher income — or to retire or semi-retire — then whatever rocks their boat is available for them to choose. Perhaps it's making that choice that stumps too many of us, so we just plod off to work five days a week because that saves us having to think about it.

So the choice is yours. Perhaps you want to chuck it all in, buy a motorcycle and travel around the world. Good for you. That's fine as long as you can handle the pay-cheque envy when your former office junior overtakes you in his new Porsche while you are doing DIY repairs on your ageing Harley on the side of the road. If, instead, you want to have it all, you could get the skills to work in a flexible industry, and then focus on working smarter rather than harder.

4

Our economy and the Kiwi obsession with property

Now we've decided that economic growth is desirable for a society as a whole, especially for the poor, and that the rest of us can opt out whenever we like anyway — we shouldn't have a problem with the government's insistence on targeting economic growth per se. Or at least, we'll have no problem unless the comfortable, no-growth lifestyle some choose to pursue is enforced upon everyone else. That's dictatorship — or possibly acute environmental activism — and no one wants that (or no one we should listen to). So we'll leave it out of consideration.

The issue then arises of how to sustain growth. We know the environment isn't an endless resource, we know we can't borrow forever to fund our lifestyle — although to look at the behaviour of many Kiwis, you'd wonder if this message has really sunk in — and we know that with short boom-and-bust growth cycles, we can end up going nowhere fast.

So the pertinent question, recognising that human beings are animals and inevitably run on the animal instincts of greed and fear, is how, ignoring economic cycles for the moment, can we get on a growth path that is a bit more impressive than the 'working harder', 'See you Sunday, Willie' one we covered in the last chapter?

We've seen that New Zealand has generally done very poorly at 'working smarter'. If this really is the holy grail of economic growth — more money with less work and less harm to the planet — how can we do more of it?

A lot of people have debated the reasons for our poor economic performance. We won't revisit them all here, but it will be useful to canvass some of the more popular ones.

A recurrent theme is that we're too small and too far away from our markets, which makes it harder for our businesses to compete and sell their stuff overseas. This is almost certainly a factor, but it's defeatist just to label it the source of all our economic woes without suggesting what we can do about it.

Another common argument is that New Zealand has suffered from a lack of *productive* investment. Basically this means we've not built enough machines and infrastructure to make our lives easier. A lot of this is historical: we have a long record of failing to invest in quality machines and infrastructure. In part, this may account for our historic inability to work smarter.

These limitations are borne out by the evidence. As you can see in the following graph, New Zealand has lower levels of *capital intensity* (think 'quality machines or infrastructure per person') than most other OECD countries. This is a significant determinant of our economic growth. If we haven't equipped ourselves with the tools we need to work smarter, we have to work longer hours instead to get ahead.

Capital intensity (OECD)

We're used to working hard. Indeed, Kiwis are renowned for it in the UK. The Poms, who fall over themselves to employ Kiwis in Britain on their OE, call it 'flogging the colonial' — they just can't get enough of these dumb-asses from Downunder who will mind shop while they head off for a long, liquid lunch on Thursday and return blearily to work on Monday.

What is it with us? Maybe we have fewer machines because we traditionally don't get great value for money from the machines we *do*

Capital intensity (OECD)

Germany
Netherlands
Italy
France
Denmark
Japan
Luxembourg
Switzerland
Finland
United States
Sweden
Australia
Spain
Canada
Iceland
Ireland
United Kingdom
New Zealand
Portugal
Mexico

0 0.2 0.4 0.6 0.8 1.0 1.2 1.4 1.6

■ MED and Treasury (2005)
► Schreyer (2005)

**Capital per unit of labour,
US = 1**

Source: Treasury[1]

have in New Zealand? This doesn't ring true, though — the return created from our investment in productive capital seems as high as anywhere, if not higher.[2]

Returning then to our question — how can we work smarter and grow our incomes? The answer seems to lie not just in having an adequate supply of savings to invest but also in appropriately allocating those savings to the right investments — those that bring home the bacon in terms of income results. Let's look at what we have been doing with our savings.

Saving ourselves

As I mentioned in *Pension Panic*, and have had occasion to repeat here, our savings rates have really been in the firing line over the past few years. The Reserve Bank governor and an array of politicians have all wagged their finger and tut-tutted loudly at our profligate ways.

It's easy enough to see how they've jumped to this conclusion. Certainly a fair few Kiwis probably don't save enough for their retirement. By 'enough', I mean they haven't saved enough if they hope when they retire to maintain the standard of living they enjoy at present. Treasury reckons that over a third of Kiwis older than 45 aren't on a savings track that will enable them to sustain their lifestyle when they retire.[3] This applies particularly to those on middle incomes — those on really low incomes are used to living off a pittance like NZ Super, and those on high incomes generally save enough. So this savings problem is facing only that chunk of households in the middle. Does this mean New Zealand as a whole has a savings deficiency?

National savings rates have been low compared to many countries, and this is largely due to recent 'dissaving' (spending more than we are earning: that is, borrowing) by households. Meanwhile, businesses and government are busily stashing money away to counteract our fetish for having the latest SUV in the driveway, flat-screen plasma HD TV on the wall, and a real blonde in bed.

In fact, the government and businesses are saving enough to make up for the dissaving by households, so the nation as a whole has a savings rate that fluctuates between 2 and 6 per cent of GDP each year. As long as our nation as a whole is saving we should be fine, no? Well, not really, argue the powers that be. We don't have enough savings to pay for all the investment we want to do as a nation in a year. This means we need to borrow the rest from overseas, which is why we have a *current account deficit*. In other words, we run a net deficit with the rest of the world as calculated by adding up our net surplus income — that is, receipts from exports less payments for imports, plus the dividends and interest we earn abroad less the same we pay to foreigners. Bottom line: we're in the red every year. In fact we last ran a surplus in this current account in 1973 — a bloody aeon ago. The graph below illustrates just the extent to which we are net borrowers from abroad.

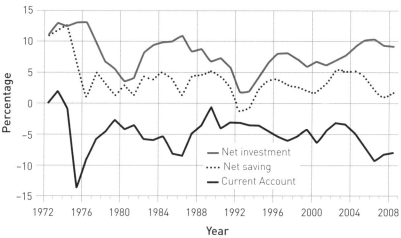

New Zealand — investment, savings and current account deficit as a percentage of GDP

Source: Statistics New Zealand, own calculations

So we need funds from overseas. Year in, year out, we need the rest of the world to top us up. They can do this by buying our assets from us and giving us a nice little cash payment, or they can just lend to us *ad infinitum*, year upon year upon year. And that's just what they do. Being so far away, they don't want to deal with tricky assets inconveniently located down in this Falklands of the South Pacific. Besides, a nice, clean debt is easier to manage than a strip of high-country sheep stations.

All those current account deficits mean that we've built up a nice store of overseas debt — as we saw in the graph on page 23. In fact, as you can see from the graph on page 62, it is one of the largest debts per person in the developed world. We're not in great company. Our neighbours on the bar graph, Hungary and Iceland, have both had to be bailed out by the International Monetary Fund (IMF) in recent times. Are we next?

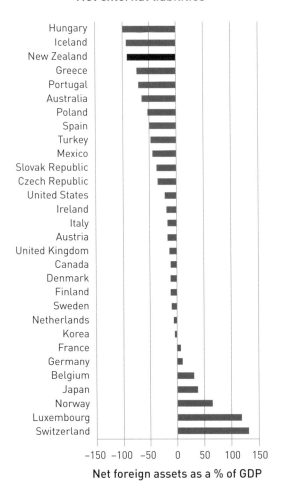

Net external liabilities

Net foreign assets as a % of GDP

Chances are you're thoroughly depressed by now, and have already started drafting a letter to the IMF begging for mercy. Financial literacy is a bugger when the news the numbers are trying to give you is so bad, isn't it? But relax for a moment. Actually looking at savings and borrowing in isolation is a little superficial, so let's try a bit harder to get to the 'true' picture.

We all know it's fine to borrow if you're putting the money into something that will give you a return on your investment. It will eventually show up in the value of our overall position — our assets minus our liabilities, known more commonly as our 'net worth'. For example, the excess of investment over savings we have seen above might be logical if the value of our assets is rising faster than the debts we owe — remind you of borrowing to invest in a house, by any chance?

Whoops. That comparison wasn't funny — we're not using the dosh from abroad to enable us to work smarter, and we're not using it to invest in assets the rest of the world currently craves. Basically, we've been shoving it into housing — *en masse.*

New Zealand — what are you worth?

As we've demonstrated above, the rate of savings isn't really at the heart of our growth malaise — that is, the need to work our butts off to get ahead. After all, we don't save any less than Finland or Denmark. So it's the results from investment of those savings that are the villain of the show. Property still dominates our asset portfolio — just look at the graph below. New Zealanders' obsession with housing outdoes just about all of our competitors.

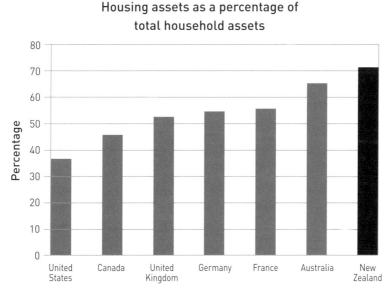

Housing assets as a percentage of total household assets

Source: Reserve Bank New Zealand

The graph below charts the growth of New Zealanders' net worth over the past 30 years (including provisional figures for 2008), as a proportion of our disposable income. Since financial deregulation occurred in 1984, we were content to let our net wealth stay at about the same level, while we steadily took on more debt. This debt largely went into housing, and the value of housing grew over the same period also — although only to the extent that we matched the growth in value with increased debt!

Then, around 2000, we got the return we all knew was there for the taking! The value of our housing assets suddenly accelerated as every man and his dog got in on the gold rush. In five years, our asset portfolio grew by 50 per cent, entirely thanks to housing. We kept raising our debt, but we just couldn't get it high enough to match the property bonanza. We're rich, rich, I tell you! Over this entire time, New Zealanders' financial asset-levels stayed stagnant — no thanks to those we charged with managing them, as we'll see in subsequent chapters. As households, our net financial assets (financial assets less debt) have plunged, leaving businesses to raise their funding increasingly from abroad.

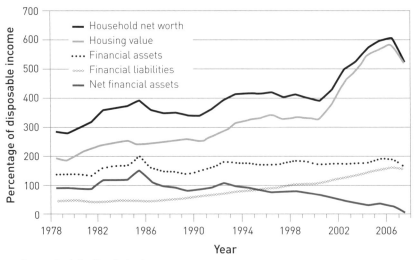

New Zealand households' net worth as a percentage of disposable income

Source: Statistics New Zealand

The increases in house prices has led to Kiwis cashing in on around 5–7c for each NZ$1 increase in the value of their house.[4] We have done this by building up debt against the increased value of our houses. Our liabilities look pretty scary, don't they, at 170 per cent of our disposable income — up from around half of our income when financial deregulation occurred in the 80s. But what happens now? House prices are falling, but our debts won't.

As we now know, the capital gains enjoyed by housing were never sustainable, anyway. There are many ways of showing this. Here's one: look at the differences that opened up between the rental return from housing and house prices. The price of most assets reflects the income stream you receive from the asset. For houses, the primary income stream is rent, so you would expect house prices and rent to grow at about the same rate. Around 2001, however, house prices rapidly accelerated away from rental incomes. This is shown by the chart below.

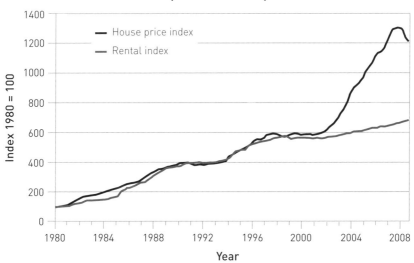

House prices vs rental prices

Source: Reserve Bank, Statistics New Zealand data (adjusted for change in Accommodation Supplement)

The upshot of this is that people were buying homes and renting them out, but the rent did not cover the mortgage on that property. In essence, landlords were paying the tenants to live there, all in the expectation of realising fabulous capital gains. The scale of this lunacy can be seen through the increasing use of *loss attributing qualifying companies* (fondly known as LAQCs). LAQCs allow landlords to run their rental property at a loss and claim the tax back on that loss. In some cunningly structured cases, that means the government is paying for up to 39 per cent of the loss on running a rental property. Between 2003 and the top of the boom in 2007, losses declared through LAQCs doubled to just under $2 billion per year.[5]

Instead of being driven by sustainable fundamentals, the rising prices depended on soaring increases in debt, a risk mostly borne by new entrants to the housing market. These 'recent' entrants (those who bought after 2002/03) are the real losers from the feeding frenzy — if they can hold on to their house, they may see negative equity for some years to come. Eventually the supply of suckers — whoops, sorry, I mean new buyers — willing to take on the crazy debt necessary to buy a house would run out as they realised they were better off renting.

But before the supply did run out, the bankers were brought to their senses anyway by the offshore credit crunch and its demolition of banks. In New Zealand, banks summarily stopped lending to suckers. The only way to keep housing prices on that sort of trend would have been a much greater stream of immigration (providing a steady supply of people to keep up demand for housing) — something, incidentally, financial-sector folk are now lobbying the government to stimulate.

The treadmill of convention

Since we're on the topic, it's probably worth saying a word about the obligation we seem to feel to buy houses — the obligation that sees the streets outside open homes of a Sunday afternoon crowded with nervous young couples pushing a pram wondering whether they'll be able to get a bid in on this one, or whether there'll be another baby boomer to shoulder them aside to add it to his portfolio of renters. Do we really need to feel that obligation?

There's a certain predictability about the Kiwi life cycle. In short, the convention is to get your education, do a few years' OE, then return, get engaged, buy a house, get married and breed. After that, all the important decisions made, you just get up, go to work, come home, feed the kids, go to bed, worry about the mortgage; get up, go to work . . . At least, this is the pattern until the last of the kids leaves home and freedom returns. Some don't know what to do with freedom by then, and they prefer to maintain the same pattern until death or retirement simplifies their day.

But along the way there are a few really big decisions, life changes that determine the shape of future years. Having children is obviously one. Another is buying that first home — the financial obligation that immediately stunts any spontaneity a young couple might previously have enjoyed. The commitment is major, and unless the timing is right, so that capital gains quickly erode the real burden of the debt, the weekly mortgage commitments can erase any freedom of choice for 10 years or more. For some couples, this can be a relationship-breaker. For others lucky enough to have timed it just before a boom, the decision doesn't even seem that major after all, at least in hindsight.

One of the legacies of the property boom that began in the mid-1990s is that we have a whole generation of young families indebted to their eyeballs in property — property they scraped every cent together to buy and paid a premium for, all for fear of missing out on their only chance to get on the ownership ladder. Such was the panic that the property bubble instilled in first-home buyers that the sustainability of the decision really never featured in their thinking — it was simply a matter of doing it ASAP. It's a panic I've seen before — the late 1970s was the last time inflation was out of control, and property prices also went on a tear. Once that bubble burst, a generation of young property owners spent a decade strung up by their mortgages as inflation was crushed and the real burden of their debts faded not one jot. It took until the mid-1990s, when the next property surge started, for them to get any kind of relief.

There's every chance that we are seeing a return to those mid-1980s conditions right now. For the moment, banks are preoccupied with keeping their funding lines open, reducing their loans to businesses stealthily, and adopting a wait-and-see attitude to housing. But with the era of fast-and-loose credit over, banks will have to revisit their property loan book and in essence tighten up. They've started by ramping up deposit requirements. What this means for the embattled high-mortgage, low-equity young couple is a period of mortgage slavery as property prices go nowhere, but the mortgage hangs around like a bad smell.

Home ownership is the Kiwi Dream, of course, but it's not the norm in many developed countries, simply because property is beyond the means of ordinary folk. And it's changing here, too. New Zealand home-ownership rates peaked at 74 per cent in 1991 and have been falling ever since, being 68 per cent at last census count. For the next few years, doing the conventional thing is going to be a prohibitively expensive choice for those conservative young families. For this to change requires either a fall of house prices relative to incomes, or an outbreak of property inflation so that buying is a no-brainer. I'd guess the former, which will eventually be good news for those poised to enter the own-your-own home ranks, but a bit tough for those who have just been there, done that.

And in the meantime? Well, renting isn't so bad when the alternative is stunting your lives and relationship with mortgage repayments. Your finances are meant to serve your quality of life, not the other way round.

KiwiSaver to the rescue

So let's get back to the core constraint on Kiwis getting the lifestyle we all see as our birthright. Our national economic problem isn't a lack of saving, it's how we invest our savings. Someone needs to convince successive governments of this, because very little has been done to change how we invest and heaps of headspace has gone into coming up with ways to raise the savings rate. The latest in a long line of government silver bullets for our saving and investment woes is KiwiSaver, our very own incentivised, voluntary superannuation scheme.

Unfortunately, as pointed out in *Pension Panic*, government savings schemes have a pretty poor record of increasing national savings. In order to entice people to save, governments around the world usually offer tax incentives for contributing to a super scheme. This is a hugely expensive carrot to toss out to people, and as a result, it heavily reduces government income. In the US, for example, these tax incentives are unlimited and tend to favour very rich Americans with high retirement savings. This, in turn, lowers the government contribution to national saving. To make matters worse, people also tend to 'offset' the increase in their retirement savings by reducing their other savings. Evaluations are mixed on the question of whether tax incentives actually increase national saving at all.

Even with a compulsory savings scheme, such as the Australian one, results are pretty disappointing. The Australian superannuation scheme was created in 1992 and the savings rate was set at 3 per cent of an individual's pay. This has been increased over time — in 2002, it had increased to a pretty substantial 9 per cent.

The increase in compulsory super contributions has had a positive impact on national saving, but it's pretty small — an increase of annual saving of about 1.5 per cent of GDP.[6] Where retirement schemes with some element of compulsion or incentive have made a difference is in the savings rates of those on middle incomes.

On the grand scale of government-backed retirement savings schemes across the world, KiwiSaver is one of the least harmful ones. It doesn't offer unlimited tax benefits to the rich, and it is voluntary. Hopefully the people that can really benefit — middle-income New Zealanders who aren't saving enough for their retirement — will sign up. Over time, KiwiSaver may also reduce the proportion of New Zealanders' asset portfolio that is sunk into housing assets. Increased diversification of our portfolio of investments will be welcome in the long term by making sure that New Zealanders don't have all their eggs in one investment basket.

However, that doesn't mean that it will increase New Zealand's annual national savings rate. It is likely that as people see their wealth build up in a KiwiSaver account, they will be tempted to neglect other savings efforts. In fact, some people may end up *reducing* their overall saving rate if they get the impression that KiwiSaver and New Zealand Superannuation alone will meet their retirement needs.

The fact is that KiwiSaver will not benefit you if you treat it as a 'set and forget' investment. Even after signing up to KiwiSaver (why not, when there is free money going!), New Zealanders all urgently need to take control of their financial future. We all need to learn how to accumulate wealth in the absence of a housing bubble, as there won't be another one of those for a few years at least. The trouble is that housing is the only investment we all understand. Even banks understand it better than other investments — just try asking the bank manager for a mortgage to invest in the share market! Broadening our investment portfolios will require broadening our knowledge. This can be tough, particularly when you start talking about investing offshore.

This process of self-education is made even harder by the swine flu infecting the financial services industry, wherein low ethical standards and lax duty of care leaves investors lying pale and bleeding from every orifice in some forgotten corner of suburbia — more on this in coming chapters. But suffice it here to ask— how the hell can Kiwis get the confidence to save and invest in financial instruments like shares and bonds etc. when we've just witnessed the most horrific financial genocide conducted on investors in finance companies and funds parading as low or even moderate risk, that have been little more than a front for gross abuse by so-called guardians of the people's money?

It just will not happen — at least not until regulators get out of bed and start designing financial markets to serve the interests of the saving public rather than those of finance company Flash Harrys and avaricious multinational fund managers. I'll spend some time in this book exposing the practices of the delightful folk that run these shops but before we finish with the present subject, let's try to understand our obsession with property and why it is we've been prepared to sacrifice so much economic growth and income in order to religiously to pursue it. We'll see it hasn't been the only indicator of grotesque excess that financial deregulation has spawned.

But property never fails

In previous books, I pointed out the perils of relying solely on housing investment for retirement savings. At the time, the usual enthusiasts, giddy after five uninterrupted years of stellar returns, were once again putting about the nonsense that property prices never fall.

Yeah, right. Tell that to anyone who bought at the peak of the market in September 2007. Official data shows that house prices have already fallen 12 per cent in real terms since then. Activity in the New Zealand housing market has fallen to its lowest level since data collection began. Leveraged investors, relying on capital gains to get rich quick, are now scrambling to cover their mortgage payments or facing up to selling for big losses. And the rot may not stop with greedy baby boomers, either. Statistics showed that in December 2008, the number of mortgagee sales — that is, where the lender is forcing the sale of the asset they took as security because the borrower has failed in their obligations to service the loan — has increased 275 per cent from the same period in 2007. For four years prior to that, the trend had been pretty flat. And whereas many of the forced sales in 2007 had been initiated by distressed finance companies, desperately trying to claw back every cent owed them before they too went bust, there has been a significant increase in the number of big, solid banks starting the process.[7]

The question is no longer whether house prices will fall — that's already happened — but by how much they will fall in order to restore some sanity to the property market. One warning sign is the ongoing meltdown in comparable international housing markets.

The international housing bust

The New Zealand housing boom was not an isolated incident. Large run-ups in house prices were a common feature in most Western economies over the 2000s. When economists start looking for the factor that kicked off the bubble, three suspects keep showing up:

▷ The big tech-wreck crash in 2001 and 2002 scared people out of the equity market, and into the perceived safety of real estate investment.

▷ The US recession, and fears of deflation, saw the US Federal Reserve cut interest rates to insanely low levels. The Fed has a strong influence on global interest rates that eventually feed into mortgage rates internationally.

▷ The 'global savings glut' — China and petrodollar countries have generated massive trade surpluses, and to stop their currencies appreciating (or because they simply lack domestic investment opportunities), those countries recycled these surpluses into lending in Western countries. This, too, pushed down interest rates.

As house prices started rising, classic bubble behaviour followed close behind. Large capital gains engendered expectations of more to come — and because property is regarded as a 'safe' asset, banks had no problems in seeing their way clear to extending generous lending conditions so long as there was some property as collateral. Borrowers thought nothing of heavily leveraging themselves, even as rental returns drifted below the rates required to service the mortgages. At the peak of the madness, US banks were making mortgage loans with teaser initial rates, even though they had a pretty good idea the borrower wouldn't be able to afford the loan when the honeymoon period was over and interest rates reset to normal. The thinking — where thought was involved at all — was that by the time the mortgages reset, rising property prices would have given the borrowers the necessary equity to refinance at more favourable conditions.

This was a disaster waiting to happen, although few foresaw how widespread the contagion would become when the housing bubble popped. Quite apart from the securitisation thing we looked at in Chapter 1, housing is such an important asset to the banking system that serious house-price falls set off a chain reaction of value destruction. Likewise, the importance of housing assets for household wealth, and the construction industry for employment, has seen the housing crash deliver a three-pronged attack on the real economy.

We've witnessed in the global financial crisis of the last 18 months just how a housing correction can become a downward spiral, with massive global repercussions. Falling house prices have pushed the thinly capitalised into negative equity, meaning the smart decision for many has been simply to walk away from their homes. Foreclosures and forced sales by the banks have had the effect of driving market prices down further, exacerbating the downturn.

But worse was to come. The destruction in the value of house prices has also eroded banks' capital — a process that was amplified by the proliferation of all those mortgage-backed securities floating around on banks' books. Soon, fears developed about the banks' solvency. Banks have had to scramble to get capital from the government to stay afloat. But in the current environment, they value self-preservation first and foremost. As a result, there's no lending going on, which means even if you still want to buy a house in markets like the US and the UK, that mortgage became unobtainable. And with no one chiselling loans out of the banks any more, there are fewer buyers — and again the downward pressure on house prices is reinforced.

House prices haven't just corrected in many of these over-heated international markets. They've tanked. The US is clearly the worst offender, with house prices now 30 per cent below the peak in real terms (see chart on the next page). But other countries haven't been immune to the housing fallout. House prices in the UK and Ireland are both more than 20 per cent off the peak in real terms.

Nor is this the end of the story! At the time of writing, for instance, US house prices were expected to fall another 15 per cent over the next 18 months. Sales remain at a very low level, and we've yet to see the full effect of the third wave of housing value destruction — that of unemployment rising sharply. Even prudent borrowers can't afford to service their mortgages if they no longer have a job.

Although the much lower mortgage rates now on offer (as central banks attempt to stabilise the housing markets) may have some hoping for brighter times ahead — that's the idea, after all — the final wave to negotiate will be the crackdown on lending standards. Regulators aren't going to want to see a repeat of the current crisis, and that means insisting on much tighter criteria for

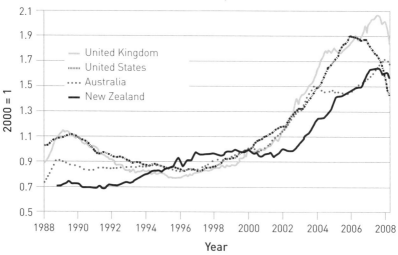

International real house prices (2000 = 1)

- United Kingdom
- United States
- Australia
- New Zealand

Source: Infometrics

lending money on housing. Many of the mortgage offers available in the boom will never come back. High deposits and steady income flows will be the new de facto standard for lending, forcing many would-be homebuyers to save again or be denied access to the property market.

Auxiliary causes of the New Zealand property boom

Are New Zealanders just punters who got sucked in by a global housing bubble? Well, no two booms are exactly alike, and New Zealanders may take some comfort from the fact that some of the recent price appreciation may reflect factors apart from low interest rates and easier lending standards:

▷ New Zealand enjoyed a substantial migration boom from 2002 to 2004, with almost 90,000 extra people arriving over these three years. The working-age population was growing by 2.1 per cent a year in 2003. Although that migration boom has since eased, we haven't seen a repeat of the large net outflows that have occurred in previous recessions.

▷ The increase in the top tax rate to 39 per cent in 2000 (since reduced to 38 per cent) made property investment, with the potential for deductible losses, more attractive to housing investors in the top tax bracket. A paper by a Westpac economist estimated that this change alone could have raised nominal house prices by up to 17 per cent.[8]

▷ Increasing council restriction on residential building, and increased standards mandated by central government, have both pushed up the cost of building a new house. This has the flow-on effect of increasing the value of existing houses (if you can't afford to build one, you're in the market to buy one).

▷ Tax incentives to invest in housing proliferate. We've already talked about LAQCs for landlords. Owner-occupiers also benefit from living in their house, because as they don't have to pay themselves rent they avoid paying tax on that rent. Another way of looking at it is this: if you had money in the bank you would get interest and you would pay tax on the interest. On the other hand, if you use the money to buy a house, you don't receive interest but you get other benefits (i.e. somewhere to live) and you don't pay tax on those benefits. In addition, there is no capital gains tax in New Zealand, making the profit from selling a home tax-free (as long as you aren't a professional property developer).

All these are good reasons to invest in housing, but the tragedy for the economy as a whole is that it has come at the expense of investment in sustainable income-generating activity. By shutting out other types of investments we have shut off the supply of money to New Zealand businesses. Worse, we have put all our investment eggs in one basket. This leaves us acutely vulnerable to falls in the housing market.

Correction or collapse?

The New Zealand housing market is substantially into the correction process, but the overseas experience, the gathering steam in the local recession, and the divergence in house prices from long-run fundamentals all stand as worrying portents of the potential for prices to crash further.

The New Zealand experience in the 1970s was one example of how the house-price correction can occur — real house prices fell by a massive 38 per cent between 1974 and 1980. It wasn't because nominal house prices were in free fall — they rose 47 per cent over this period. It was just that inflation rose a whopping 138 per cent at the same time! In real terms, house prices didn't recapture that previous peak until December 1995 — that's a real return of 0 per cent a year over 21 years! Who says you can't go wrong with bricks and mortar?

The more recent housing market slump at the end of the '90s was milder, but similar in form. Real house prices fell 7 per cent from 1997 to 2001, reflecting a mere 2 per cent drop in nominal house prices combined with a 5 per cent increase in inflation.

There are two points to take away from this. First, house-price corrections tend to be long-lasting affairs. It is unrealistic to expect that New Zealand house prices have finished their downward correction, or that a recovery is right around the corner. But there will be false dawns along the way, as those convinced that the boom times of the last decade will be back with us in a jiff. These 'suckers rallies' will simply elongate the inevitable adjustment back to normality.

Second, inflation is normally the grease on the wheels of the house-price adjustment. But in a period of low inflation as we have now, it is much harder to achieve a price correction in this manner. If prices are to return to fundamentals, ongoing nominal house-price falls will be required.

The advantage of an inflation-driven correction is that it erodes the value of the mortgage as well as the value of the house — meaning that although house prices are falling, borrowers are not losing the positive equity they have in their property. Nominal house-price falls, on the other hand, do erode that equity, meaning that householders are more likely to end up 'underwater' on their property. This puts us on the path to the US dynamic of a downward cycle in house prices, where borrowers with no equity default, and mortgagee sales further depress house prices, driving more people into negative equity.

And from a psychological perspective, real house-price falls are probably easier to accept when they occur through the 'invisible' process of inflation than through a stark lack of demand and a trickle of tightwads at your open home crossing out the zeros on your asking price.

So how much further do house prices have to fall? This is the multibillion-dollar question for New Zealanders and their housing wealth — and the banking system that depends on house prices not falling into a hole.

The run-up in house prices after 2002 is highly conspicuous in relation to the long-term trend. Even after a 12 per cent fall, it would take another 20 per cent fall in real prices (either through falls in house prices or erosion by other inflation) to return to trend the trendline. If the process of correction is drawn out, then such a fall doesn't have

Real house prices (Index, March 2000 = 1)

Source: Infometrics

to happen, the trend will catch up. I'll tease this out more in the final chapter, but we can see that other crashes ended with house prices a further 20 per cent below the trendline from the graph.

Comparing house prices to household income further underlines the growing affordability problem. House prices were on average 3.5 times the average household income for 30 years between

1974 and 2004. Even after recent falls, they are up at 5.2 times average household income. And using household income as the denominator ignores the fact that households have tended to move from one to two income earners over this period. Hence far more working hours are required to afford a house. With the prospect of rising unemployment, income growth will be relatively muted in coming years, making it harder for this ratio to improve without house-price falls.

However, there is one ray of hope for the housing market. In an effort to rescue the economy — and the banking sector — the Reserve Bank has slashed interest rates to historic lows. And with floating rates down at 6 per cent, the Reserve Bank has engineered a

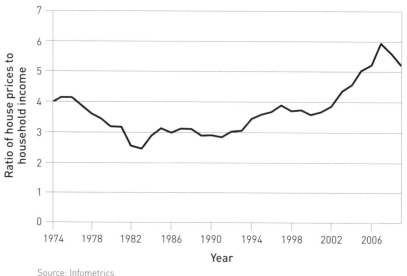

Ratio of house prices to household income

Source: Infometrics

temporary recovery in debt-servicing ratios, meaning that someone on the average wage should be able to service a mortgage on today's elevated house prices — if interest rates stay low forever.

That's a big if! Most economists think that a neutral Reserve Bank official cash rate is around 5–6 per cent, not the current 2.5 per cent. Anything lower than that, and inflation will, eventually, start to accelerate out of control. So today's low interest rates could well

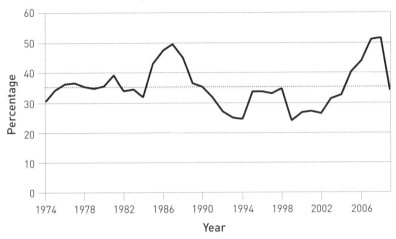

Mortgage servicing as a percentage of household income
20% deposit, 25 years, floating rate

Source: Infometrics

be a once-in-a-lifetime, never-to-be-repeated offer, and shouldn't be relied upon (in other words, fix soon, for pity's sake, and for as long as possible).

But even low interest rates can't prop up the housing market if banks are unwilling to lend. The credit crunch has done away with the glory days of mortgages on 5 per cent deposit, and banks throwing money at their customers to get into property. That 20 per cent deposit hurdle is now the real constraint on entering the property market, and lower interest rates won't change that.

It's hard to escape the conclusion that another 10–15 per cent fall in real house prices is about the most optimistic 'correction' that homeowners can hope for. That might sound alarmist, but it is in fact a conservative forecast with respect to the international experience. A recent paper by Kenneth Rogoff and Carmen Reinhart examined housing market crashes in the wake of financial crises.[9] On average, real house prices fell by 36 per cent over six years. And the current credit crisis would appear to fall towards the severe end of the range of crises examined in that study.

We've all been quick to point the finger at banks and regulators for creating this current recession. But that begs the real question: are we *all* to blame for the crisis? After all, the banks simply gave us the rope we asked for, and from which we're now dangling.

Executive pay — another bubble waiting to burst

Property hasn't been the only sector to have seen wild excesses as the consequence of fast-and-loose credit. From the financial deregulation of the early 1980s, it's been the burgeoning of the financial sector that has underpinned the various booms we've encountered — particularly in tech stocks and now in property. Well, they've gone bust. And one bubble that has yet to burst is the explosion in executive pay.

The remuneration of chief executives has skyrocketed in line with the debt ratios in the economy — and as we'll see, this hasn't been a coincidence. As the graph below shows, it was the norm up until the early 1980s for CEO pay in the US to be around 30 times that of the average worker. That peaked at 300 times in 2000 at the end of the tech boom, before retreating of late to a more modest 260 times!

And what have shareholders received as a result of this?

The graph illustrates that since 1993, when executive remuneration

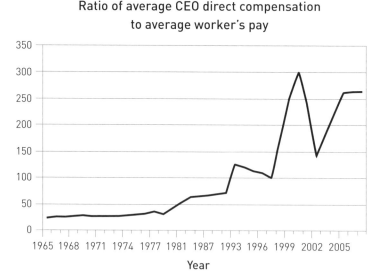

Ratio of average CEO direct compensation to average worker's pay

Source: Economic Policy Institute

really started to take off, the earnings of the corporate sector enjoyed a golden run that emphatically ended in tears. In other words, these highly paid managers managed only to expand shareholder wealth in a

Real earnings growth, S&P500 (5 year moving average)

Source: Infometrics

transitory manner — the value-add that they delivered in return for their ridiculously inflated salaries was the debt-drunk era of leverage. Since financial deregulation of the early 1980s, the finance sector has been at the forefront of the largesse — see the graph at the top of the next page.

And what has happened to debt since the managers were able to assemble their own pay packets? Well, the best indicator of that is what's happened globally in terms of the big imbalances between saving nations and borrowing nations — see the graph on page 36 in Chapter 2. In other words, all these highly paid managers have achieved is to load the economy up with debt and drive it to the wall. In New Zealand, where — lest we forget — funding our lifestyle with other people's funds has long been a way of life, as evidenced by the graph on page 23 in Chapter 1, our debt has just become a larger and larger burden. And we've been obliged to sell off more and more of our productive capacity to pay our bills, as the second graph on page 82 illustrates.

The share of what's produced in New Zealand that's now the property of foreigners has lifted from about 3 per cent of GDP to

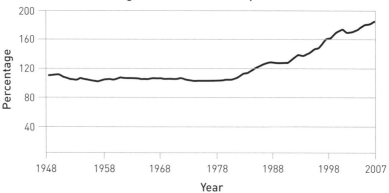

Pay per worker in the financial sector as a percentage of average United States compensation

Source: http://www.theatlantic.com/doc/200905/imf-advice

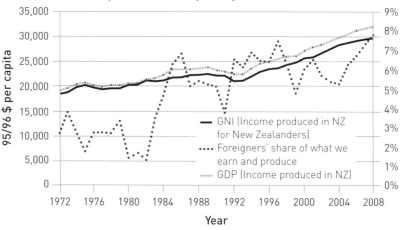

How much of what is produced in New Zealand do we own? Comparison of real per capita GDP to GNI

Source: Infometrics

8 per cent. So no matter which way you look at it — the burden of our foreign debt or the share of the income produced in New Zealand that is not ours — the consequence of those years of giddy excess continues to grow.

The unavoidable conclusion is that highly paid CEOs have done little but subtract rather than add value for shareholders, and the phenomenon of soaring CEO pay, which we've seen in New Zealand too, has just been symptomatic of the orgy of excess that a leveraged economy permits. In short, it has been a grab by management for the value that enterprises create, at the expense of shareholders and the rest of the employed workforce.

Examples abound, but there's been a tendency for control of large public companies to move from the shareholder base to management. In large part, this has come about because enterprises have become so large that it has been less and less likely that any single shareholder or concentrated group of shareholders have been able to exert effective control. Rather, it has been the norm for investment funds to become the largest shareholders on the register, and while in theory these funds are agents for their own investors, they don't usually show the kind of interest in the companies they have a stake in that leads to boardroom activism. Institutionalised shareholders tend to vote with their money. Once they decide the company is not for them, they sell, otherwise they stay, maybe trading around the edges depending upon their own net fund inflows.

This leaves effective control of such a public company, apart from in times of corporate crisis, to the management. Even the board's effective ability to represent the interests of shareholders is diluted when management and existing board members can control appointment of directors. And that rise of executive power has been manifest in corporate behaviour — CEO pay is just one example. But the ability of senior management to help itself to the company's resources hasn't been restricted merely to fat remuneration packages and the issuing to themselves of easy-peasy 'in-the-money' options packages. It's also been clear in the ability of management to collude with one or two strategic shareholders to defend themselves against unwelcome advances from would-be outside investors.

It's been a common tactic, for example, during these years of easy credit for managers to load a company up with debt in order to deflect unwelcome attention from outside shareholders. When a company mounts a takeover action against another, a typical reaction — whether in the interests of minority shareholders or not — has been the 'poison pill' defence of debt-loading to discourage the potential suitor. With the onset of the credit crunch, those poisonous tactics have blown up in their promoters' faces with a vengeance. Banks and other creditors have tightened the terms of loans and suddenly the company finds itself having to sell assets in a weakening market to cover the debts it's taken on, leading to a severe weakening of the balance sheet and, in some cases, insolvency. Of course, in such cases it's not just the management that is hurt, but all shareholders. A very high price is paid by shareholders for having allowed managers to seize effective control from the owners of the company.

The alienation of the interests of shareholders from the conduct of companies has been a feature of the boom and is likely to result in either a weaker market for publicly listed shares, or a reassertion of control by shareholders over the company they collectively own. The failure of the funds management institutions *en masse* to act as effective agents for shareholders will be a consideration investors take more seriously as they look to place their hard-won savings after the global recession ends.

But let's look next at another key reason our savings and investment sector is failing to offset our spendthrift tendencies, namely the gross inefficiency of the funds management and financial advice sectors as a wealth-creating machine. And why is the very industry we look to for the solution turning out to be a very large part of the problem? Well, as someone once wrote, something is rotten in the state of it.

5

Professionals managing money badly

Carrying on from the theme of the last chapter, New Zealand doesn't have a savings problem so much as a problem with achieving effective investment of those savings. In this chapter, we'll take a look at the role played by the investment professionals who manage New Zealanders' savings, and perhaps we'll start to understand some of the reasons why (up until recently, at least) every mum-and-dad investor held it to be indelibly true that, *'you're better off doing it yourself — you're better off buying property'.*

The track record of investment returns for Kiwis placing their savings in savings products is, as we shall see, very poor. Over the long term, they haven't even made a market average return, which suggests one of two things. Either ordinary Kiwis are financially illiterate and suckers for punishment when it comes to investing their hard-won savings with the financial sector, or it is the investment management industry, dominated in New Zealand by multinational insurance companies, who have done New Zealand savers no favours. And if you're scratching your head over the answer to that one, here's a hint; it's the latter.

Let's start by illustrating the investment performance of just three groups of professionally managed funds that together account for around $50 billion of New Zealanders' savings:

▷ superannuation funds

▷ the 'Cullen Fund'

▷ KiwiSaver

Superannuation funds — long-term losers

Many New Zealanders are making the effort to save. Superannuation schemes of one sort or another are a surprisingly popular method of doing that saving. In fact, around 690,000 New Zealanders have a superannuation account with their name on it. They may not know what's in it, who's running it, what it does with their money, or what fees are being charged on it. But they know their money is out there, somewhere, doing something . . . They hope that their money is well managed. They hope it's safe. As with most things financial, when all else fails, there will always be hope.

The superannuation industry is fragmented across 550 schemes that together manage $28 billion, but the largest 75 schemes, which have in excess of $50 million each, account for 85 per cent of the funds, so that is where we have concentrated our investigation.

Our conclusion isn't reassuring. Generally the industry utterly fails to add value; in fact, it's worse than that — it damages the retirement prospects of New Zealanders. And we've further concluded that this is because:

▷ performance is poor

▷ transparency is low

▷ fees are high

Private superannuation schemes come in two stripes — the employer-based schemes, which commonly see not just employees making contributions from their wages, but their employers making a contribution for their staff as well. Then there are the retail schemes, which are promoted mainly by the big multinational life insurance companies and are open to anyone. Generally, people join these when they're buying life-insurance products from these companies.

In both cases, however, the ultimate managers of the schemes tend to be the same group of foreign players — and of these AMP and CBA (through subsidiary Sovereign) from Australia, AXA from France, ING from Holland, and Mercer and AON from the US dominate the industry. The banks are also active in the space, with Australia's NAB (through its subsidiary BNZ) being a player.

Before we delve into the employer-based and retail schemes, let's consider how these long-term savings schemes are typically structured. Such schemes comprise the following — a trustee, an advisor/consultant, an administrator, and a number of investment managers. The roles can be mixed and matched and the same entity can perform more than one of them. This can give rise to some disturbing conflicts of interest, as we'll show.

▷ The savings/investment scheme: The bulk of the public's savings with the financial sector are invested in funds promoted by the large multinational life insurance conglomerates that dominate the New Zealand market. These companies have evolved from pure life insurance businesses and deploy many of the techniques they developed for life insurance endowment policies to control the fund — savers are treated as unsecured creditors, and 'reserving' is used as a device to separate savers from their property.

▷ The trustee: Charged with looking after the interests of the scheme and, in theory at least, the interests of the members (i.e. savers, contributors or unitholders). But the trustee cares for the members *as a group*. It has no fiduciary duty of care to an individual contributor. In the event there's a conflict between the interests of one member and other members, the trustee will rule in favour of what is best for the wider group.

▷ The advisor/consultant: Though sometimes engaged and paid by the trustee of the scheme, the role of advisor/consultant is more commonly played by the promoter and manager of the scheme, especially in insurance company- or bank-run schemes. The advisor/consultant is charged with translating the investment mandate into an asset allocation and, quite often, with selecting fund managers (fund of fund-style schemes being the most common in the New Zealand context). It's by no means uncommon for the advisor/consultant to choose divisions of the same firm as fund managers. The advisor/consultant is also there to provide expert advice to the trustee when called upon, and is therefore often used as a defence for poor performance — it provides a fallback for inexpert trustees, who can legally say 'we took professional advice' and wriggle off the hook when called to account for poor decisions.

▷ The investment managers: In the ubiquitous but opaque fund-of-funds model, sector specialists are usually selected by the consultant. Of course, in bank- or insurance company-promoted schemes, the promoter is usually simply running a feeder fund for various fund managers, trading on its own retail reputation as a bank or insurance provider to generate a commission. Not that the investor would know: transparency in this kind of arrangement is usually minimal.

▷ The administrator: This role is to provide the interface for savers to contribute, withdraw funds, make requests and monitor performance. Often with bank-or insurance-promoted schemes, the administrator and the advisor/consultant are one and the same.

If the fund manager were simply caring for each individual saver's property, then the supply chain would be much shorter. The manager would simply contract to care for the funds under their management for a fee, without laying any kind of claim to property entitlement in those funds. The aggregated funds would remain just that — everyone's individual savings pooled for the purposes of being invested — without being turned into a fund with a separate legal entity.

But the contemporary model interposes a *discretionary trust* between a saver and their money. All that legalese in the offer documents might look as though it's there to protect you and your money, but in fact, it's achieving the opposite. Its effect is to gently prise your property from your grip and place it beyond reach.

Further, conflicts arise when a single firm performs more than one of the roles listed above. The conflicts arise for two reasons:

▷ There is this pretence that the trustee somehow knows what they're doing — which in the case of employer-based schemes is seldom the case; the trustees are generally well-meaning folk drawn from the ranks of the employer or employees and they rely totally on the expert advice of the advisor/consultant, or perhaps one of two 'expert' independent trustees. Generally such teams are far from expert in their role of watchdog over flash finance types executing the provisions of complicated legal documents. The same goes for charitable organisations — bastions of the community the appointed trustees may be, but financially literate they mostly are not. So to discharge their duties, they become totally dependent on the advice of the appointed expert. But of course, the advisor is hardly the most reliable source of advice on the propriety of its own activities! I think we call this a conflict of interest. It gets even worse if the firm that acts as advisor also supplies one or more of the selected fund managers — again, far from uncommon in this industry. And even where it's a bank- or insurance company-promoted scheme and the trustee can be presumed to be an expert, you still can't count on them to represent your interests, because as I've said their obligations are all to the fund, not to you, the individual member.

▷ The lack of transparency forces the saver/investor to rely on this chain of representatives to do right by them. As we've explained, from the trustee down, the duty of care is to the fund as a whole and not to the individual saver. The individual saver is dog tucker.

An approach that promoted full and continuous transparency would overcome much of the deficiency of the unit trust-type investment product. I'll talk more about unit trusts in general in the next chapter.

Employer-based schemes

The graph below shows the performance of some of the largest workplace-based balanced schemes. Our performance measure takes into account the contributions made into each scheme by both employees and employers and all data is net of tax and fees, so we are focusing solely on the performance of the investment managers — asking how much value they add.

We include two standards by which to compare the performance of these schemes: a market index of 50 per cent world shares and 50 per

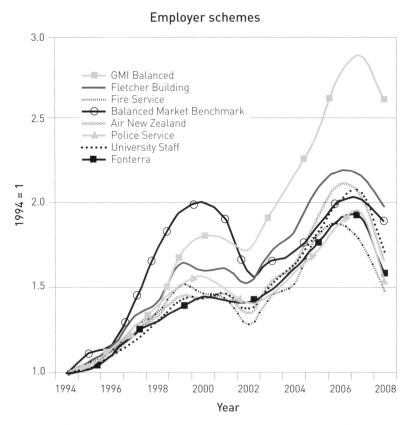

Source: The performance lines on the graph are the returns we extracted from the material given to us by investors and/or employers. Thank you all for your help.

cent New Zealand government stock, and the track of GMI Balanced, the balanced portfolios from my own funds management company, Gareth Morgan Investments Ltd. Both standards are adjusted for tax and fees, so they are comparable.

The alarming result is that only one of these large employer schemes has beaten the market-average benchmark and that is the Fletcher Building Retirement Plan. Well done! The rest, in other words, haven't added value at all; they have detracted from it. The Police Service and Fire Service, Fonterra, Air New Zealand and university staff schemes appear to be particularly awful in this regard.

To put the graph into perspective, the average fireman (invested in the balanced option) made just 2.9 per cent per annum after tax and fees over a 14-year period. That's significantly below a balanced market benchmark and has only just outstripped the cost of living. In other words, $1.00 invested in 1994 has turned into $1.48 by the end of 2008 or just $1.09 in real terms (that is, adjusted for inflation). There were alternatives available that would have turned that dollar into $2.60 — that's how much our fireman has missed out on. And even if he had enjoyed nothing more than average market returns (so had no value-add from his investment manager at all) his $1 invested in 1994 would now be worth $1.85. Our bevy of multinational life insurers that sit behind these schemes provide no value-add for New Zealanders. Who are these firms that the trustees of these employer-based schemes are relying on? The table on the next page provides a glimpse.

When you see the commonality in this table it's not too unreason-able to leap to the conclusion that the *en masse* underperformance that I outlined in the earlier graph is an unsurprising result given the common supply chain of 'helpers'.

I'll talk more about trustees in the next chapter and how, from the perspective of individual saver/investors, they can impede rather than encourage progress. For now, it will suffice to recall what I said earlier that the trustee is responsible to the fund rather than separately to each and every one of its members. Not only does the trustee have no obligation to the individual saver, but it's a sad reality that the real focus of many in this role is to ensure that they don't have any liability whatsoever.

	Fire Service	Police Service	University Staff	National Bank Staff	Westpac Staff
Advisors & Investment Managers					
Mercer Super Investment		✓	✓		
Melville Jessup Weaver	✓			✓	
Russell Investments Group		✓			
Fund Managers					
Alliance Bernstein NZ	✓			✓	
AMP Capital Investors	✓	✓	✓	✓	✓
ING NZ Ltd	✓	✓	✓	✓	✓
NZ Asset Management	✓				
Tower Asset Management	✓	✓	✓		✓
BNZ Funds Management		✓			
Arcus Investment Management		✓			
BT Funds Management		✓			✓
Brook Asset Management		✓	✓		✓
Mercer		✓			
Western Asset Management		✓			
Tyndall Investment Management NZ		✓	✓		
PIMCO		✓			✓
Westpac Investment	✓				✓
Administrators					
Mercer NZ	✓	✓	✓		✓
Jacques Martin	✓			✓	
Watson Wyatt NZ	✓				✓

Source: An example of those who are (and have been) involved in the superannuation sector, by scheme, from annual reports

Individual trustees don't have limited liability, and so any utterance or other communication they make to a member can be used against them personally. This has the predictable consequence of making most of them more concerned with arse-covering than with anything else — such is the cross to bear for members of employer-based schemes.

And apart from the trustee's freedom to do little more than preside over the exploitation of individual member saver/investors, there are a number of other faults with the most commonly used trust structure that makes it worse than useless.

▷ Placing a trustee in charge can be significantly inferior to the situation where a saver/investor has a direct relationship with a professional funds manager. When the trustee is not a professional — as is commonly the case with employment- and charity-based schemes, for example — each newly appointed trustee comes to the governance role with no memory. They're like children in need of schooling. Contrast this to an individual client, who, so long as they're provided the relevant information (seldom does this occur, sadly), finds their financial literacy growing with experience. An important part of an advisor/client relationship is the client's confidence and financial literacy that is built up over time. Dealing with trustees who have different agendas is no substitute.

▷ Trustees aren't experts, and so they defer to professionals. This is a legal defence against charges of incompetence, but such a cop-out should not be available, as it is the trustee who has the fiduciary duty, not the expert. Trustees who can't rely on their own expertise to make the relevant judgment calls should not assume that duty. Certainly, they shouldn't be in a position where they need to rely on the investment consultants and administrators sector, which is incestuous, self-serving and utterly devoid of concern for the interests of individual investors.

▷ And it's not just experts that trustees will defer to. They also keep a weather eye on what the pack's doing, so as not to stray too far from the track of the benchmark set by their consultant. This leads to stale governance at best. I have commonly seen the inadequacy of the trustee model revealed when I hear trustees object to a fund manager's suggestions, saying, 'I would never invest my own money this way.' It may sound like prudence, but all too often, the difference is born of the fear of departing too far from the 'norm' for trustees. This creates a spiral toward a mediocre and homogeneous level of investment expertise, and this inevitably is expressed in fund performances. The graph on page 90 of fund performances doesn't conflict with this conclusion.

In short then, fund trustees, no matter how well-meaning and con-scientious, add little value. Not only have they been shown, in too many cases, to have singularly failed to protect the interests of individual savers/investors in unit trusts and superannuation funds where the manager has skimmed funds from individual savers, made advances on softer-than-market terms to related parties and in general lined their pockets at the expense of clients, but they can also provide an impediment between the professional investment manager and their ultimate client.

And whereas they are supposed to serve as guardians of the money that is separated from its rightful owners by unit trust structures, they are both willing and able to dodge any kind of fiduciary responsibility for contributors' funds. Why bother with them at all?

The regulatory and institutional deck is stacked heavily against the interests of the individual saver/investor and it is here where reform is most urgently required. Effective reform will eliminate the role for deadweight links in the chain and ensure that it is fiduciary care for the individual saver/investor that is paramount.

Let's look at the Police Superannuation Scheme simply to illustrate and try to understand the extensive layering that sits between a member and their money. The trustees of the police scheme hire Russell Investment Group as their advisor, who assist the trustees in monitoring the administrator, investment manager and specialist investment managers. With me so far? Good, because it gets worse. The first table on the next page shows the 'specialist investment

Asset class	Investment manager
Australasian shares	Brook Asset Management & ING (NZ)
International shares	Mercer (Mercer overseas share plus fund)
Global property	AMP Capital Investors & ING (NZ)
Alternative assets (commodities +)	Western Asset Management
International property	AMP Capital Investors & ING (NZ)
NZ fixed interest	Tyndall Investment Management NZ
International fixed interest	PIMCO
NZ cash	ING (NZ)

International equity managers (Mercer Overseas Share Plus Fund)	
Alliance Capital Management	Arrowstreet Capital
Baillie Gifford & Co	Bernstein
Edinburgh Partners	Taube Hodson Stonex Partners
Acadian Asset Management	State Street Global Advisors
Lazard Asset Management	

managers' who are selected by the investment manager (in this case, the Mercer Super Investment Trust).

Unfortunately, the police scheme is burdened with yet another layer of investment managers! The second table above shows the investment managers used by the specialist international shares manager.

So just to recap: the trustees talk to the advisor, and they both talk to the administrator and investment manager, who then selects the 'specialist investment managers', who manage the buying and selling of assets controlled by still more investment managers ... Phew! I think you get the idea. No wonder individual clients can't assess their own investments — there are just too many layers of bureaucrap interposed between them and their money. And the palms of all these little helpers need to be greased too.

Instead of having one investment manager, some super schemes have five, and some have 27. No kidding: 27! Then you need someone to manage the managers, and the managers that the managers have hired — stacks and stacks of paid help. Investments can benefit from some oversight and feedback, but only up to a point. Beyond that it doesn't matter how many layers of management you employ, your investments won't be any safer, or gain value any faster, but they will sure as hell cost more.

Just as an example then, we've established that individuals in the Police Superannuation Scheme are having their investments managed to death, but as we've also seen, that doesn't mean the police scheme will outperform the market average. In fact, quite the contrary: it seems to have resulted in consistent underperformance. This scheme is a bomb — nothing unusual about that though; there are many out there.

The poor cousin — retail superannuation schemes

If you think workplace-based superannuation schemes in New Zealand are a rip-off, you haven't seen anything yet. Retail superannuation schemes — those where any financially illiterate fool can be readily separated from their money — are where the foreign life insurance multinational conglomerates really get to bleed New Zealand savers dry. The Government Actuary reports on the total performance of each sector and the results are presented in the graph opposite.

As the graph on page 97 shows, both the retail and employer-based schemes have trailed the benchmark market return for a balanced fund, although retail schemes are markedly worse. As the underlying managers are the same, we can only conclude that, free from the scrutiny of workplace-appointed trustees, the financial 'services' sector is free to wreak havoc upon the hapless retail investor. In other words, one of the benefits of employment-based schemes is that their bargaining power has reduced the fees chopped out of an individual's account. The difference in performance is about 1.6 per cent per annum.

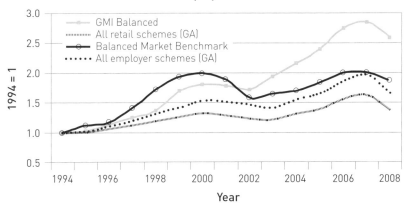

Retail vs employer schemes

Source: The line denoting the average return for all retail and employer schemes is produced from published Government Actuary (GA) data. The results for the 2008 calendar year are estimated from Eriksen's published Master Trust Survey, as GA data is yet unpublished.

Trustees of superannuation schemes consistently tell their members that their money is doing well: reading their annual bumf mailed out to members, that is the party line. However, the graph clearly shows that generally this is not the case. The trustees aren't scoundrels but the road to hell is paved with good intentions, and unfortunately, the sad reality is that the status quo is so entrenched that trustees these days struggle to focus on the simple things that matter: transparency, benchmarking and cost.

We've seen that it's a rare workplace super scheme that makes market average returns — generally they make substantially less than you could throwing darts at the board down at the stock exchange. We have also hypothesised that the schemes offered directly to the public are being punished by additional fees — not an unreasonable deduction, given that the underlying managers are the same. The next graph (see overleaf) illustrates in more detail just how bad the retail schemes are.

There just isn't a large scheme out there offered to the retail investor that has a track record of making even market-average returns. Remember the poor fireman whose $1.00 invested in 1994 was worth a lousy $1.09 today, 14 years later, in real terms? Well, if he'd put the dollar directly into Sovereign superannuation it wouldn't even be worth $0.99 in real terms! How much punishment do New Zealand's savers

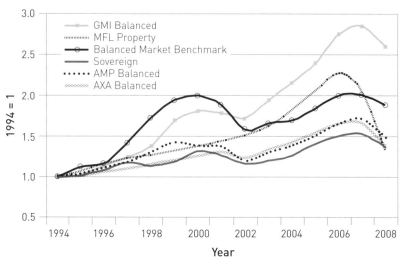

Retail super schemes

Legend:
- GMI Balanced
- MFL Property
- Balanced Market Benchmark
- Sovereign
- AMP Balanced
- AXA Balanced

Y-axis: 1994 = 1
X-axis: Year

Source: The performance lines on the graph are the returns deduced from material given to us by investors and from publicly available data — thank you all for your help.

need to take before they recognise big brands and big marketing budgets don't equate to a good deal?

There's no doubt that the offerings from the cabal of foreign providers are hurting the prospects of New Zealanders in retirement. It's nothing less than a crisis, which confirms the general observation that New Zealanders *are* making lousy investment decisions. Nobody is forcing us to be suckers.

Schemes for government servants — send in the clowns

Indeed, in May 2009, Morningstar International released a report that described the New Zealand funds management industry as the worst of all the countries it had surveyed. Depressing as all this is — and remember, there's around $50 billion of New Zealanders' savings sitting in superannuation and other big funds — let's continue to rake over the toxic waste that the superannuation industry leaves in its wake.

Over the years, several attempts have been made by the government to solve the superannuation problem for government servants. Once upon a time, government servants belonged to a guaranteed benefit scheme first introduced in 1948. This gold-plated beauty proved too expensive even for hardened politicians to pass the look-yourself-in-the-mirror test. The investment managers — the same old ones who have bludgeoned New Zealand savers in the retail and workplace-based schemes outlined above — have been so adept at making below-market returns, that promises to guarantee government servants payouts based on market-average returns have proved to be utterly reckless. The politicians had to rescind this undertaking and in 1995 they closed the scheme to new members — but not before accumulating $8 billion in liabilities that have to be covered by the taxpayer. The scheme currently has 17,000 contributors and 47,000 annuitants with $3.5 billion under management.

Even though it's closed, it's still a big scheme on the New Zealand superannuation landscape, so it's worth taking a look at. From the point of view of those in the scheme, it's a good thing that their benefit isn't connected to the performance of the investment manager, as yet again, the industry is failing to add value.

For the employees of local authorities and government quangos, the old superannuation scheme was the National Provident Fund — another of these gold-plated taxpayer-guaranteed funds, thankfully now closed. The 11 remaining NPF superannuation schemes are unique in New Zealand, as they are government-guaranteed, which means members are guaranteed a certain benefit or minimum return on their retirement nest egg. That's all very well, but when the investment manager inevitably fails, the rest of us pick up the tab.

For example, the meat industry has an NPF scheme that guarantees members a 4 per cent per annum return. At first glance, 4 per cent per annum sounds simple enough to achieve. But surprise, surprise! The scheme has 12 different investment managers — oh dear, here we go again — and over the 2008 financial year, the scheme returned just 0.11 per cent.

The NPF schemes run reserve accounts (which in themselves are a highly dubious practice, as we'll explain in Chapter 6). For example, in 2008 the Meat Industry Scheme 'topped up' those who were leaving at the expense of those remaining behind. However, the real test for the NPF schemes is going to be at the end of the current financial year. The credit crunch has pushed them to the brink. Will they have enough money in their reserve accounts to cover the gap between their investment losses and the guaranteed benefit? If not, they will go cap-in-hand to the government and the taxpayer will pay for the incompetence of the schemes and their investment managers. Thankfully for the rest of us, NPF schemes were closed to new members in 1991.

When the Government Super Fund was shut down to new members, its cudgels were taken up by the Global Retirement Trust (GRT). It's a rare thing for a government to learn something, but in the case of the GRT, they did at least try.

What made the GRT different was that it was set up as a New Zealand-owned, not-for-profit superannuation vehicle. 'Not-for-profit' sounds good, but in practice it is difficult to cull bureaucracy with more bureaucracy. So although the scheme did cut out some cost, they still had the usual raft of advisors and investment managers sucking on the teat.

When the GRT was shut down to new members in 2004, the GRT 'teamed up' with Mercer and performance has headed back down below the balanced market benchmark.

Continuing with this circus of superannuation for government servants, in 2004 the government introduced the State Sector Retirement Savings Scheme (SSRSS, 40,000 members and $400 million), also now closed to new members after a very short half-life. Within the SSRSS, members could choose to have their savings

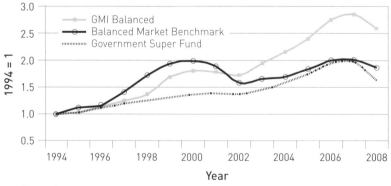

Source: Annual reports

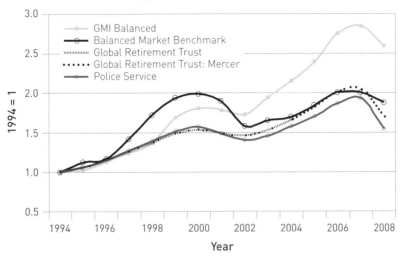

Global Retirement Trust

Legend:
- GMI Balanced
- Balanced Market Benchmark
- Global Retirement Trust
- Global Retirement Trust: Mercer
- Police Service

Y-axis: 1994 = 1 (0.5, 1.0, 1.5, 2.0, 2.5, 3.0)
X-axis: Year (1994, 1996, 1998, 2000, 2002, 2004, 2006, 2008)

Source: Annual reports, members supplied information

managed by one of our three foreign favourites — AMP, ASB or AXA. Giving credit where it's due, although AXA and ASB have failed dismally, AMP has outperformed the balanced market benchmark over that time.

These days, new government servants just join KiwiSaver as their workplace superannuation.

We've looked at the schemes introduced by the government over the years, and although they come in different colours and stripes, they all have one thing in common — underperformance. Once again, returns haven't even matched market averages, so there's a good reason for both members and the taxpayer alike to be dissatisfied. Employer contributions go some way to obscuring investment manager failure, but a failure it certainly has been.

The Cullen Fund — monkey see, monkey do

The NZ Superannuation Fund, aka the 'Cullen Fund' (because it was the brainchild of the Minister of Finance in the Fifth Labour Government, Michael Cullen), is the largest superannuation fund in the country. Since the fund's inception, $13.5 billion of taxpayers' money has been put in and now we only have $11.8 billion left. But it's a Clayton's fund — one that claims it's a superannuation fund, yet isn't anything more than money set aside by government that it alleges it will use to partly fund National Super for the over-65s when the hordes of baby boomers pass that magic, pay-me-now date. The reasons I call it a delusion include the following facts:

▷ No government can bind the actions of a future government with mere promises;

▷ Already, the new National Government has indicated that it could use up to 40 per cent of the Cullen Fund to finance projects in New Zealand — hardly an approach calculated to deliver specific payments to national superannuitants;

▷ The performance of the managers of the Cullen Fund has been atrocious, meaning that any rational contributor — in this case, the government, which spills in $2 billion per annum — would be having second thoughts about backing this turkey;

▷ It was a dumb idea from the start, as several of us shouted from the rooftops at the time of its inception. What matters, when the time comes to write big cheques for the baby-boomer masses, is the ability of the government to pay the bills on the day. And that is driven by the performance of the whole economy, as reflected in its tax take at that time. To try to deny that reality by relying on the funds-management industry is a sick joke, born of a tragic naïvety on the part of Michael Cullen that somehow fund managers add value.

For how much longer a government desperate for funds to help rescue an ailing economy can keep its hands off the remaining $12 billion is the quiz of the day.

Over the five years since the fund was formed in 2003 (until the end of December 2008), it soared to a value of $1.035 for $1.00

invested on Day One — compared to the market-average benchmark return for a balanced portfolio that is now up to $1.13.

Curiously the fund benchmarks itself against a risk-free rate of return, which it defines as the New Zealand 90-day bill rate. Such a comparison is curious — considering the fund is 80 per cent invested in growth assets — but it tells us much about how its managers see the world.

> The performance objective of the fund as a whole is to exceed, before New Zealand tax, the return on treasury bills by at least 2.5 per cent pa over rolling 20 year periods.
>
> New Zealand Superannuation Fund

The term '20-year rolling periods' is the key here. Our trusty Cullen Fund guardians expect that over this period, growth will always win out and they'll secure at least their 2.5 per cent per annum premium for every period. Oh dear. I think they've been reading too much of the industry's propaganda. Consider the following. The twentieth century (or any century, for that matter) can be divided into 88 rolling 20-year periods. Half of the 88 periods over that century produced compounded returns of less than 4 per cent — and that's before tax! So even with 100 per cent in the stockmarket, 50 per cent of the time our Cullen Fund would have failed its own test — and by reducing the stockholding to the 80 per cent it currently owns it probably would fail by even more, albeit with less volatility period-to-period.

The point is the guardians don't know what they're doing in setting the benchmark — it sounds very much like industry-bluff parading as an authoritative undertaking. With an 80 per cent allocation to growth assets, all they can responsibly undertake to do is fulfil their aim to perform better than an 80/20 stocks/fixed interest benchmark. They haven't got a clue what the actual returns will be.

This highlights one of the major shortcomings of the funds-management industry. We foolishly think stockmarkets have been around for aeons and we can conclude much about the future from their recorded past. But since 1900 there have only been five separate and independent 20-year periods, actually. That is a small sample from which to make bold statements about 'the long run'. Yet the industry professionals mouth off about the prospective returns as though they actually have an historical basis for their prognosis. Any Statistics 101 student would tell them such prognoses are vacuous. I'll look at this in detail in Chapter 7.

Anyway, the guardians have made their bed, so now let's have a look at the state of their sheets. The cumulative performance of both the Cullen Fund and the 90-day bank bill is shown below (after tax and fees):

Having launched into the fair-weather winds of a bull market, the Cullen Fund has bombed at a rate that parallels the awful, no-value-add of its contemporaries destroying wealth hand-over-fist in the private superannuation industry. Having been an ill-conceived concept from the start, the fund has shown itself now to be just another sick puppy from the superannuation sector that deserves to be put down.

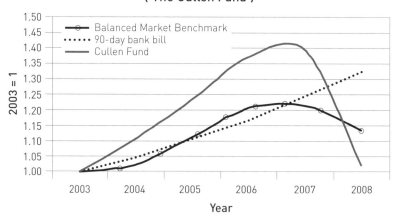

New Zealand Superannuation Fund ('The Cullen Fund')

Source: New Zealand Superannuation Fund data, our calculations

The Cullen Fund employs 27 separate investment managers, not to mention numerous investment advisors and consultants. Why be merely inefficient when you can be super-inefficient? To the average person on the street — the builder, nurse, doctor, plumber, shopkeeper, farmer and truck driver — slogging away making the dough to fuel this money-go-round, such layering and the absence of any value-add is a drain on their net worth that should be isolated and exterminated.

Not surprisingly, the expenses of this monster are too high, at roughly 1 per cent of funds under management (FUM).

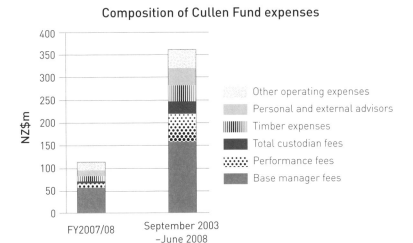

Composition of Cullen Fund expenses

Legend:
- Other operating expenses
- Personal and external advisors
- Timber expenses
- Total custodian fees
- Performance fees
- Base manager fees

X-axis: FY2007/08, September 2003 –June 2008
Y-axis: NZ$m

Source: New Zealand Superannuation Fund Financial Report 2008

Expenses:
$136.4 million for 06/07
$113 million for 07/08
$350 million from 03–08.

For a fund this large, expenses as a percentage of FUM should be way lower — of the order of 0.5 per cent maximum.

It goes on. Do you notice anything wrong with the assets owned by the Cullen Fund, shown in the table on page 106?

Cash. Here we are in the midst of the biggest economic meltdown of modern times, and this team is holding virtually no cash. Now, notwithstanding the fact that this is a long-term fund, and also that it has cash top-ups every year from government, to blindly sink everything into assets that are falling in value as we go into the largest sell-off since the Depression is curious to put it kindly. It just looks like the same old hoary industry convention — the markets will see us right in the end. I bet if these guardians had their own money on

Asset class (31 Dec 08)	Value ($M)	% FUM
New Zealand equity	830.7	7%
Private equity	166.9	1%
International fixed income	1,613.2	13%
New Zealand fixed income	76.9	1%
Global listed property	748.8	6%
New Zealand listed property	318.2	3%
Commodities	615.0	5%
Infrastructure	890.2	7%
International equities — large cap	3,913.3	33%
International equities — small cap	702.7	6%
International equities — emerging markets	321.3	3%
Timber	1,255.0	10%
Cash	593.2	5%
Total	12,045.4	100%

the line they wouldn't so readily espouse the buy-and-hold, set-and-forget industry mantra. Nor would they be happy with 1 per cent expenses on this amount of money.

Stunned-mullet investing of this order is enough reason in itself for the government to stop throwing good money after bad.

KiwiSaver

There are KiwiSaver schemes galore — 54 at last count (January 2009). On the face of it that's great for savers, because it gives them real choice. Moreover, an open market encourages new players to put up innovative schemes, and goodness knows the funds-management industry could do with some fresh blood. However, a new and potentially juicy market is a magnet for some providers more interested in lining their own pockets than providing people with innovative and responsible long-term savings schemes.

For you the question is whether you can tell the difference. If you can't, or can't be bothered, don't moan when you finally wake up to the reality that KiwiSaver funds are not government-guaranteed, they can underperform and they can go bust. Financial illiteracy isn't an excuse for allowing this to happen to your money.

Some providers are so specialised that one would have to wonder what the authorities were thinking to allow specialised funds as KiwiSaver schemes, given the whole point of KiwiSaver is to offer a prudent, long-term savings vehicle for mums, dads, Jacks and Jills. There's one scheme that currently invests solely in commercial property, others that offer nothing but 100 per cent invested in shares, and several that confine themselves to investing solely in New Zealand or Australian shares. Now, specialist funds are fine, but there is a time and place for everything. And KiwiSaver is not that place. A KiwiSaver member has all their Kiwi-savings in just the one scheme (you can only be in one scheme at a time).

The default providers

There are six default schemes that the government chose and to which they can direct members who either don't know which provider to go with, or who just can't be bothered choosing. The default providers are primarily the same big foreign institutions that have dominated the funds-management industry for decades and delivered the distinctly underwhelming investment performance covered earlier in this chapter.

Many people who have allowed themselves to be drafted to one of the default providers will find themselves in a default investment product. The default product for these providers has been prescribed to a large degree by the government and is at the conservative end of the risk spectrum — low volatility and commensurately low real returns.

Despite the appalling performance of the default schemes, they have been successful in attracting members. Marketing dollars and size have triumphed over rational choice, as the graphs on page 109, depicting the performance of the six default providers plus Westpac, show. Remember ANZ and National, as well as a number of the smaller KiwiSaver providers, have investment management done by ING. Once again, the GMK (Gareth Morgan KiwiSaver) results are not there just to show off. While we're the only other provider with more than $100 million in KiwiSaver funds under management, there are a number of smaller providers that have delivered results similar to or better than GMK's. I've used ours as indicative of the others, because I can state ours with complete confidence.

The graphs indicate the investment returns for the major providers over the year ended February 2009. The percentage figures can be interpreted as the dollar losses or gains on every $100 invested at the beginning of the period.

The investment results for the big institutions reflect their mechanistic approach to investment strategy. For instance, members choosing 'growth' seem to have had the majority of their contributions invested in shares no matter what was happening in share markets — no tactical *nous* permitted!

KiwiSaver was designed to make it easy for people to save for their retirement. It has also made it easy for a whole raft of people to set up KiwiSaver schemes and an even bigger group of commission-fed people (insurance and mortgage brokers and the like) to sell KiwiSaver schemes to the public. All great stuff, but like any new financial product in the market, the fringes are populated by some pretty crackpot providers and dodgy white-shoe salespeople. KiwiSaver is no exception. Clearly the regulatory authorities aren't capable of policing the fringes of this market. That highlights the need for Joe and Jill Public to get themselves up to speed with what to be wary of in a KiwiSaver provider. The smarter Kiwis prove to be in picking suitable providers, the less likely the lunatic fringe is to survive.

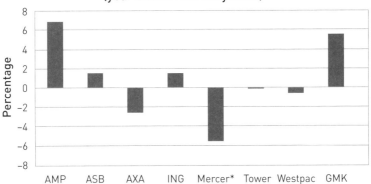

KiwiSaver Conservative Fund returns
(year ended February 2009)

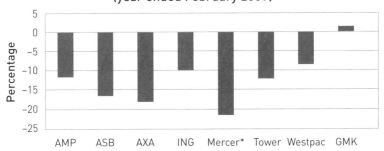

KiwiSaver Balanced Fund returns
(year ended February 2009)

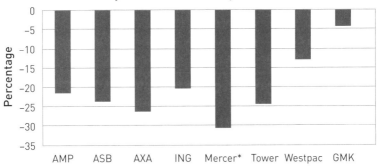

KiwiSaver Growth Fund returns
(year ended February 2009)

Source: FundSource data published in *Weekend Herald*, 4 April 2009*

* Mercer returns are from its Feb 2009 Monthly Report adjusted for tax.
Returns data are for the year ended 28 Feb 2009.
All returns are after fees but before tax.
GMK — Gareth Morgan KiwiSaver, returns published on www.gmk.co.nz.

6

The financial services sector — a place to abuse savers

The last chapter illustrated how poor the performance of various funds operating in New Zealand has been. The bottom line is that, in the main, the funds-management industry does not add value — indeed, it measurably detracts value. In any normally functioning market, such a situation would only be short-lived; competition would ensure that investors were offered alternatives that exposed the incumbents as inadequate by comparison and the investors would vote with their feet.

Yet the poor performance seems to persist year after year, the perpetrators continue to attract monies and the investors keep getting pummelled all the way to retirement when they 'discover' it's all been one great tragedy. The obvious question is why?

There are a number of reasons the malfunction persists. Here are just a few, one for each of the clients, the providers and the regulators:

▷ Financial illiteracy — investors in many long-term savings schemes are denied access to the appropriate information that enables them to make astute decisions, and as a result remain so financially illiterate they cannot differentiate between an infomercial and relevant, vital data on the fund they have invested in. Most fund reporting is long on general market conditions and almost devoid of any useful, investor-specific information.

▷ Obfuscation — this industry specialises in perpetuating an 'information asymmetry' between itself and its clients. The most significant example of this is the universal deployment of *unitisation*, which ensures a client cannot see what securities they are invested in, has no way to independently validate the valuation the investment provider publishes, cannot determine whether there's a margin hidden within the unit pricing mechanism, and cannot verify the transactions carried out on the client's funds over any time period.

▷ Regulatory inadequacy — this covers a host of sins and lapses on the part of those charged with supervision of this industry, but foremost among these is the separation of investors from their property, viz., their funds. Unit trusts and superannuation schemes are separate legal entities that enable those charged with their management to pursue interests quite in conflict with those of individual members or investors.

And so it goes on. There's a litany of shortcomings in efficiency in these products that have enabled their promoters to gouge, short-change and mislead investors while the regulator stands aside, totally ineffective. It has been an absolute Eldorado for the industry and its hangers-on, in the form of consultants, actuaries and, on occasion, even trustees, who have collectively aided and abetted what amounts to a very serious infringement of investors' property rights.

Let's elaborate.

Unit trusts and superannuation schemes — devices easily manipulated

To a large degree, institutional and regulatory arrangements favour the issuers of savings products at the expense of investors. At the heart of this anomaly lies an (incorrect) acceptance by regulatory authorities that the practice of pooling the monies that clients invest in unit trusts and superannuation schemes — the same thing as the legal separation of savers from their property — is neutral to the investors' interests. This is far from the truth. Rather than fund and money managers acting as custodians of an individual's property (their savings), they construct separate legal entities that become the legal owners of the property in their own right, albeit with a concomitant liability to the investor. In other words, by placing their savings into pooled funds such as unit trusts and superannuation schemes that have a separate and distinct legal identity, the investor becomes little more than an unsecured creditor of that entity.

It's this separation that underpins the industry's ability to exploit investors and disregard their interests for their own pecuniary advantage. The managers, investment consultants and scheme administrators act in concert in the interests of 'the fund' (and themselves), and far too often to the direct disadvantage of the individual saver, whose rights and redresses end up well down the pecking order — indeed, pretty well last in line, in some cases. This situation is about as far from being legally obliged to have a fiduciary duty to investors as it's possible to get.

The natural injustice of this situation is aided and abetted by the regulatory framework and its guardians, who design laws and regulations that promote the interests of these funds in a manner that is quite contrary to the interests of an individual member investor. Politicians, regulatory actuaries and policy advisors seem to be ignorant of the reality that what is in a fund's interest isn't necessarily in the interests of an individual member, and indeed, can directly harm a member. From the day they invest until the day their portion of the fund is restored to them — when the fund winds up, or they are able to redeem — people lose sovereignty over their property. How many investors realise this when they sign up to a unit trust, a managed fund or a superannuation scheme?

And how many people realise that this is all true of KiwiSaver schemes, too? Your contributions to your KiwiSaver account are placed in KiwiSaver superannuation schemes that have a distinct legal entity; in other words, you have no choice but to surrender sovereignty over your property, and must rely upon effective monitoring of scheme behaviour and ethical standards to prevent actions that are not in your individual interests. In light of the way KiwiSaver has been set up, and the likelihood that it will dominate the long-term savings sector over the coming decades, there's an onus on regulators to ensure there's no perpetuation of the inequity and worse that has become a time-honoured tradition in the unit trust and superannuation sectors. Each of these sectors supposedly operates under the watchful eye of the Government Actuary and Securities Commission. We wouldn't hold our breath for KiwiSaver to remain safer or cleaner than the long-term savings schemes that have gone before it.

Let's look at a couple of typical examples of how it is that managers of funds act in ways that are contrary to the interests of individual savers/members — ways that just couldn't occur if no legal separation of people from their property was permitted.

Example 1: Reserving policies

It's common for funds to set aside some of their members' savings 'in reserve' for anticipated liabilities that the fund might encounter. It's important to know that the minute your savings are transferred to reserves you lose right of ownership over them — they're now in a pool that belongs to the fund, and it's from this pool that 'reserves' are cut out and ring-fenced. You may or may not be entitled to get your share of that money back upon your exit. It depends entirely on the discretion of the trustee.

Let's say 10 per cent of your savings are hived off into reserves to meet some future tax liability that the fund may or may not encounter. Then a couple of years later, the liability is adjudged at, say, just 60 per cent of what was set aside — or 6 per cent of your then savings total. But say you've left the fund in the interim and moved on. The question is what happens to the 4 per cent of your then savings that was put into the reserves but for which there is now apparently no need?

The first thing to understand is that there is no obligation on the trustee of the scheme to hunt you down and give your 4 per cent back! Ultimately, there are two possible scenarios with that money. The 4 per cent is redistributed across all current members when it is released from reserves, in what we call an 'intergenerational transfer' between scheme members — you've been screwed but other members have benefited from your misfortune — so it's not all bad.

Or secondly — and believe us, this happens heaps — since you left, the scheme has been deliberately wound down by its promoter/manager (that friendly, big-brand life insurance multinational) to be replaced by a new scheme that is far more 'modern, competitive and attuned to the latest investment market conditions'. So members have been encouraged to transfer from your scheme to another and of course if the unused reserves haven't yet been released to members then they stay behind. Eventually there might be only a few members left so the manager/promoter recommends to the trustee that those members be given a *pro rata* share of the unused reserves but that the rest of them be designated 'free reserves', a nice windfall left for the enjoyment of the manager/promoter once the scheme has been closed. Nice work if you can get it — and such injustice is de rigueur in the multinational life insurance-dominated industry that promotes itself, and is accepted by incompetent regulators, as the conventional or mainstream savings sector.

The vast majority of KiwiSaver schemes are designed to accommodate reserving policies. The regulators so far would have us believe that this facility won't be abused. Given the appalling track record of these same regulators to protect the interests of individual savers in standard superannuation products, such reassurances are worth little.

Example 2: Closing redemptions

In *Pension Panic* I talked about the risk — mostly theoretical — that unitisation poses to the property rights of investors. Since that book came out, sadly, there have been plenty of practical demonstrations of the various ways in which unitisation is designed to favour the provider at the expense of investors.

How often over the last year or two have you woken up to hear the morning news bulletin declaring that such and such a fund has suspended redemptions due to 'unfavourable market conditions'? And it's not just those too-good-to-be-true funds that have been honestly promoted to the investing public as wildly speculative but potentially hugely rewarding.

In fact, it's been quite the opposite — in the main it has been funds taking in money from the public and promising them a set yield until maturity: a fixed-interest fund, if you will. The 'fixed-interest' aspect tends to be reassuring, giving the fund the appearance of a slightly souped-up bank account — paying a little more, but still essentially safe and dependable, unlike more volatile and risky investments, such as shares. The public can be forgiven for having been sucked in by this misrepresentation. They can also be forgiven for asking why, if their fund was a steady, conservative investment option, has it been suspended?

That this kind of thing can go on is unforgivable on the part of the regulators, who should know far better than to allow an equities investment to be promoted as fixed-yield. Mutton dressed up as lamb is still mutton, even to the modestly discerning palate. Yet the naïve investing public has paid dearly for the regulatory lapse that has enabled so many charlatans to dress up their speculative offerings to mum-and-dad pensioners as a steady, safe, fixed-interest option.

Indeed, one of three big-brand multinational banks that operates here even had its tellers recommend to customers that they move funds from their bank deposits into a safe-sounding 'Diversified Yield' product that was, to listen to the pitch, no more risky than a turbocharged term deposit. This disgusting misrepresentation still has to fully play out. The arrangement between ANZ Bank and its 49 per cent-owned ING NZ insurance company managed to well and truly stitch up a whole lot of savers who simply and stupidly trusted these brand names, solely because they do heaps of advertising.

Here's a since-published excerpt from an ANZ Bank advisor to a customer, dated September 2006, promoting the ING Diversified Yield Fund:

> This news does however give you one last opportunity to invest new money into an account that returned 10.42 per cent for the year ending 30 June 2006. This is a low risk, highly diversified account (with your funds spread over some 12,000 individual investments at present), which does not contain direct equities, property or finance company debentures.
>
> *Sunday Star-Times*, 29 March 2009

This letter was quite blatantly attempting to mislead the person who received it, misrepresenting the product as 'low risk'. The mere fact that ANZ was seeking to sell a product on behalf of a third party, and presumably for a commission, should have attracted the attention of the Reserve Bank, given how beyond the pale of normal practice that is for banks.

Banks, of course, enjoy the privilege (implicit, until it is tested by the market, whereupon it quickly becomes explicit) of a taxpayer guarantee of deposits. And yet, contrary to the position of responsibility in which this places the bank, condoned by the board and apparently sanctioned by the Reserve Bank, the ANZ proceeded to sell this dross under false advertising — until the market called them on it. The fund was suspended in March 2008.

It seems amazing, if you're inclined to have any faith whatsoever in the regulatory regime, that no sanction has been imposed, even after the exposure — it's simply left to those who have been misled to pursue their own remedy, at their own cost. This is a good example of just how far behind the eight-ball our regulatory regime is and why it engenders so little confidence from the public.

Let's look at the case of the suspended ANZ/ING Diversified Yield Fund a little more closely, because it can also illustrate for us the real iniquity of the unit trust structure. Consider the damage done to individual investors as this fund approached oblivion. Those who were sufficiently informed and interested to do some digging would have discovered that the ANZ/ING Diversified Yield product actually had a major investment in the spiralling CDO (collateralised debt obligations — a close cousin of the mortgage-backed securities we've already met) sector. That would have set the alarm bells ringing and the switched-on investor would have quickly put in a redemption request from this fund.

In a collapsing market such as we've seen with CDOs, it's always the case that investors are slow to recognise just how fast their holding is becoming worthless. So ANZ/ING would have done the conventional thing and valued their CDO holdings at 'latest trade' price. The redeeming unitholder then would have got that value — whether or not the fund had any real chance of selling those CDO holdings for the estimated price. In other words, rather than go to market immediately and sell all the holdings that the redeeming member had claim to and then hand over the cash realised, the fund would have valued them at latest trade and paid the member out from the cash float that unit trusts typically hold to pay out redeeming members (to avoid spending all their time going to market with the fiddly, often unmarketable parcels of shares that comprise the individual's holdings). Even if the daily trading in CDOs was thinning out dramatically, as potential buyers were scared off by the emerging crisis, the fund would still regard the prices struck on such trades there were as representative of the value of their holding. This is unrealistic, of course, because in this situation (and in many comparable situations) there would be no way to offload their entire holding at such prices. With demand drying up, the real market price would undoubtedly be much lower, perhaps even zero. But that wouldn't stop the fund proceeding with the whole valuation fiction.

As more and more members cash out, two inequitable effects are visited on the remainder. First, as each member takes their cash and runs, the assets that comprised their holding are reallocated across the remaining members. This looks fine while the unrealistic 'last trade' value is used to calculate unit prices. But meanwhile, the concentration of toxic assets in the portfolios of each unitholder is building up, especially if the fund sells down holdings of sound assets to generate more cash. And second, when finally the fund's cash float is exhausted, it has no option but to begin liquidating its assets, whereupon the full extent of the difference between the 'last trade' value and the real market value, under fire sale conditions, becomes terribly apparent.

Eventually what happens is that the trustees of the fund have to face up to reality — they have invested in a bum asset and now people want to liquidate in a situation where there is no or minimal market value for that asset. The trustee has to make a decision: to write the asset down to zero and tell unitholders that's the true market value of their holding, or to suspend redemptions/withdrawals from the fund until 'market conditions improve'.

The fair and honest course of action is the first one. It's the latter approach that ANZ/ING decided to take with the Diversified Yield Fund. Only time will tell whether the trustee has got it right in suspending transactions and locking investors up as it has done.

The convenience (for the manager) of the unit trust structure comes at a very high cost: the loss of control of one's property. There can be no starker illustration. This is the critical flaw in such devices as unit trusts, a flaw that their promoters certainly don't highlight and of which the regulators seem content to remain blissfully ignorant.

The whole seedy process leading to the catastrophic finale has been grossly unfair on unitholders: some have got out at valuations that have not been validated by a market transaction —instead, they've been guesses approved by the trustee — while others are now locked in and can't get out, even if they're prepared to wear the market price for the distressed assets. And how cruelly ironic it is that in its flailing about to preserve the fund's viability, the trustee will have made the unitholders the less-than-proud beneficial owners of even more of these distressed assets than was originally intended. The thing to do, if the trustee were truly serving the interests of the investors rather than 'the Fund' and its promoter, would have been to liquidate the impaired asset at market prices or, if this was not possible, value it at zero. This, at least, would ensure everyone was treated equally. As soon as estimates of values are relied on then a unit trust structure will guarantee that not all investors are being treated fairly.

What should be done?

At a minimum, valuations of units should never, never, never be in the hands of the promoter, manager or trustee of the fund. Their interests in no way coincide with those of the individual unitholder. Second, if unitisation is going to be used, then an independent valuer should be compulsory and this person or people must have regard only to the interests of individual unitholders, considered separately and not as a group. This means it's not just the prices of underlying assets of the fund that have to be tracked, but far more importantly, any changes to the allocation of units to any individual's account. In other words, the valuer has to be in a position to certify that the fund trustee has not made decisions that benefit or potentially benefit one unitholder or group of unitholders at the expense of others. Remember, the trustee is appointed to look after the interests of the fund as a whole, not of each and every individual member. When you join one of these things, the trustee has no fiduciary duty of care to you as an individual investor in the way that, say, a lawyer would do if you gave them money (the deposit on your house, for example) to place in their trust fund until you required it.

Of course, to comply with any requirement for this kind of continuous, independent verification would be incredibly onerous. It would be better and more pragmatic to outlaw unitised funds altogether. They are so opaque, they have such an undistinguished history of unit mispricing practices, that they won't be missed. While they claim — quite falsely — to allow small investors who wouldn't otherwise be able to do it to access a diversified portfolio of difficult investment avenues, these claims turn out to be true only under very specific market conditions — conditions that are seldom met. Most of the time, the alleged benefits to the small investor are more than offset by the horrific cost — the loss of sovereignty (control) over their property, and the fact they're at the mercy of the trustee who is *not* charged with treating each and every member equally or equitably.

The stresses the difficult market of 2008 has placed on all investment products has shown up unit trusts for the toxic dross that they really are. Any sense of fiduciary duty their guardians, let alone their promoters, might feel toward you, the investor, is so hopelessly diluted as to be useless. Worst of all, the individual saver simply loses all control of their property. Unit trusts — or more precisely, collective investment vehicles — need to be banned.

Implications

Even without KiwiSaver, the banning of unit trusts and the restoration of the sovereignty of investors over their savings would have profound implications for the investment scene in New Zealand. But the existence of KiwiSaver — a long-term savings vehicle — makes it just that much more urgent, as unit schemes dominate the KiwiSaver market. The opacity of unitised products to the saver is not only a major hindrance to the raising of citizens' financial literacy, it cripples what might otherwise function as a valuable, independent check and balance on the providers' information. As it stands, the saver has no choice but to trust the system. This is unacceptable and unnecessary.

There's no reason a pooled investment cannot separately identify every security or part-security owned by every member and communicate that information continually to each member. This would enable each member to check transactions on their account and, where possible, to get independent verification of the values the fund manager has adopted. It's a very important quality control process and one that the regulators ought to be championing, given how long this industry has witnessed a horrific lack of ethical standards.

There would be certain practical inconveniences associated with doing away with unitisation, and some costs. Full liquidity could be impaired or delayed while unmarketable parcels of equities or securities are dealt with, but the alternative is an unacceptable loss of control for members over their entire portfolio investment — far too high a price to pay, far too much trust to place in their provider. And lately, we've seen schemes offering full liquidity suddenly locked down, and the property rights of their investors suspended, pending further notice. Which, then, is the worst of the two evils?

KiwiSaver is a long-term savings vehicle, a wealth-building option for New Zealanders. The government needs to overhaul its structure urgently to ensure it doesn't become yet another way for providers to enrich themselves at the expense of their clients. It must ensure investors individually have full transparency and as much control as possible (within the limits necessary in a long-term savings vehicle) over their property. The present system is morally wrong and poses an extreme financial risk for savers.

Fund of funds and opacity

Many unit trust offerings in New Zealand are of the fund-of-funds type. We've been talking about the dubious practices that can and do go on behind the veil of unitisation. The year 2008 will be memorable also for demonstrating that unit trusts can also hide the activities of unscrupulous operators who set out purely to swindle people. The Bernard Madoff scandal, wherein it appears US$50 billion of funds contributed mainly by feeder funds — such as the unit trusts that proliferate in New Zealand — was nothing more than a pyramid scheme. Redemptions were simply paid out of funds coming in, and no investments even took place! The manager of the fund got away with this fraud for so long because there was no transparency — investors can't independently verify what's happening with their money. This point is critical — with regulators allowing, and indeed endorsing, structures that are so opaque they have done the consumer an evil, even though their job is supposedly to protect the interests of the consumer.

On the New Zealand scene, many retail funds are little more than feeder funds to those operated internationally by the banking and insurance conglomerates that advertise and heavily market their brands here, paying so-called 'financial advisors' commissions to flog their products. (The sham that is the financial 'advisory' industry in New Zealand is discussed in Chapter 8.) Because of the obfuscatory structures permitted in retail funds in this country, it's absolutely impossible for our regulators to reassure investors that their savings aren't being skimmed and misappropriated at various stages along the supply chain. The situation is totally unacceptable, and drastic overhaul of our regulatory regime is long overdue. More on that at the end of this chapter: but let it suffice for now to point out that the present protection of the savings industry establishment is not in the public interest.

Fund manager awards — another example of self-serving industry sham

Once a year, the funds-management industry in New Zealand gathers for an annual self-congratulatory love-in, showering awards on itself and basking in the wide, infomercial-style publicity that goes with the territory when you're hailed with such sobriquets as Fund Manager of the Year, Financial Planner of the Year, Investment Advisor of the Year, and so on. A cursory examination of the process — the sponsorship and criteria of these awards — soon reveals just what a sham they are: self-serving for those involved and concocted by the industry to mislead the public. Read on.

Let's take the annual FundSource awards for the 'Fund Manager of the Year'. You'd naturally think that this is bestowed on the firm that its peers consider to have performed with the greatest distinction that year. But it costs money to enter these awards: only those managers who believe the publicity is worth the investment will enter.

What's more, once a winner is announced, they have to pay FundSource (a local 'investment analysis' company owned by the NZX) for the privilege of using the endorsement in an advertisement, and it's not cheap. Apparently it costs the winner $30,000 for that right and the runner-up $10,000. That's why this awards ceremony amounts to nothing more than a circus put on for the big players so they can pay a fee to self-promote by parading some allegedly independent accolade.

Not that the winners will let on about the dosh they've handed over; as we've seen, transparency and openness are not this industry's strong suit.

The stone cold fact is that the Fund Manager of the Year award is a commercial arrangement that is of mutual benefit to the winner and to FundSource, no matter that the public is led to believe it is somehow authoritative, independent and that the winners are meritorious.

Here's a sample of the drivel FundSource peddle to the public when they make their annual announcement:

> Nomination for the FundSource Awards requires the fulfilment of a rigorous set of criteria, including a disciplined approach to investment management, the ability to retain skilled resources across various asset sectors and the ability to deliver consistent performance. The winners are then selected on their ability to deliver superior risk adjusted performance relative to their peers. All the elements within the Awards are embedded within FundSource's ongoing qualitative and quantitative research process made available to fund managers and financial intermediaries.

Let's look at the list of past years' winners:

2008 ING

2007 Tower, ING second

2006 ING, AXA second

2005 Tower, ING second

2004 Tower

2003 BNZ Investment and Insurance, Tower second

2002 BNZ Investment Management,
      Guardian Trust second — 6 nominees

2001 BNZ Investment Management, Tower second

Does it seem to you that a small number of firms scoop the awards, year after year? Proof of excellence? Or could it be that paying $30,000 to show off the award is actually not seen as either ethical or worth it for most fund managers? After all, who is supposed to pay for all this? Could it be . . .? No, surely not. But yes! The savers (again)!

And just look at the list of glittering winners more closely. Why, there's our old friend ING, who turns out to be a 'prolific' winner not just of the FundSource award, but also of the equivalent gong dished out by rival 'analysis' house, Morningstar. This would be ING, New Zealand's largest fund manager — the same high-minded, deeply trustworthy institution that (along with ANZ playing gumshoe salesman) managed to convince thousands of New Zealanders to move their money from bank deposits into the 'conservative' Diversified Yield Fund, which has now suspended redemptions and at last count had fallen some 70 per cent below par due to the high-risk gambles it took. Not only did FundSource unblushingly accept ING's payments to publish its awards and to award the Dutch insurer its highest accolade in 2006 and 2008 (plus a bevy of runner-up awards), but Morningstar saw its way clear to award this same company its principal award every year from 1993 to 2006. What a prescient judge of fund reliability Morningstar has turned out to be — I'm sure all those who have invested on the back of Morningstar's accolades will be so pleased. And now, in May 2009, we have seen the latest act in the tragicomedy that is Morningstar, with their announcement well after the fact that they've discovered New Zealand has the worst funds management industry of any nation they've surveyed. That horse was over the horizon long before their analysts even thought to close the stable door.

We'll have more to say about ratings agencies shortly, but suffice it to say here that their conflict of interest is total. They earn their living by being paid by the fund managers that they rate and publicly disseminate their findings. It's analogous to commission salesmen who purport to have the public believe they're advisors. In the US the Securities and Exchange Commission is investigating the ethics of credit ratings agencies for the same practices these fund ratings agencies deploy. The public needs to be aware that industry awards are anything but markers of excellence. Rather, they are meaningless indicators leading one to question whether that's due to innocent rating agency incompetence. It's an ethical issue — and once again, the regulator's out to lunch.

7

Theory versus practice — the good, bad and downright disastrous approaches to portfolio management

Chapter 5 highlighted how poorly big investment funds in New Zealand have performed over the recent past, while in the last chapter I elaborated upon one of the drivers of that ongoing horror story — the device that divorces savers from their savings. That estrangement via separate legal title permits gross abuse of savers' property rights by the investment and savings industry.

But quite apart from the damage via malfeasance within the industry, it suffers from another plague — incompetence. There's a yawning gap between the theory of good investment practice — how to achieve the best possible returns subject to investors' specific tolerance for risk — and how professionals actually go about that in the New Zealand funds-management industry.

The theory of building wealth-preserving portfolios is well established and is the foundation upon which investment advisors and fund managers should construct portfolios for clients. Unfortunately, in far too many instances, clients' money ends up in structures that have precious little to do with the client's tolerance of risk and appetite for reward. The reasons for this can vary, and include the following:

▷ The advisor and/or fund manager is just inept. Many in the financial advisory industry are product salesmen with inadequate skills in establishing and designing portfolios suited to individual investor preferences.

▷ The funds-management industry employs legions of managers whose priority is to deliver returns within a strict range of the market average — lest they personally get castigated for taking on too much risk. This gravitation to mediocrity, or 'hugging' of the market index, condemns clients to wealth destruction as we have seen during the 2008 credit crunch. If a share market is going to fall 40 per cent for instance, an 'index hugger' will stay fully invested all the way down.

▷ The remuneration of most advisors is commission-based and derives from selling specific products only. So clients are fitted out with something off the rack, no matter what their tolerance of risk or appetite for reward is. This seldom works when buying a suit; it's hardly any more appropriate here. The remuneration for fund managers is inextricably tied to the quantum of the funds under their management — especially when they're small, as many of our individual funds are — so their priority is on marketing their fund rather than ensuring its performance.

▷ The advisor's or fund manager's index-constrained system is very slow to adapt to changes in the investment environment, and clients find themselves locked into yesterday's products and over-weighted in sectors that are well past their best, long after the advisor or fund should have responded to changes in the market.

▷ In some cases, where the advisor's remuneration does have a large performance-based component, it can happen that in an effort to make greater personal income, the advisor places too much of clients' money into high-risk/high-return products — thus violating the client's tolerance for risk.

These are just a few of the traps that lie in wait for the unsuspecting public when they hand over their hard-won savings to the financial services industry. But let's begin this chapter by laying out the basics of building a savings-preserving portfolio that will build value over time in a manner consistent with your tolerance-of-risk/appetite-for-reward.

Investment basics: How to do it

1. Controlling specific risk

There are two types of risk in a portfolio. The risk specific to individual assets or classes of assets (shares, bonds, cash, or currency, for instance) that you include in your portfolio relates to the risk that one of them may go belly-up, for example. Companies do go bust (remember the dotcom days?) and you can lose all the dough you've invested in them, but so long as any one company is just a small portion of your whole basket, you won't lose your shirt.

One of the tragedies of the 2008 financial collapse has been the number of investors whose lifetime savings have gone up in smoke because they failed to take enough heed of specific risk. The example you will have heard about is those poor folk whose advisors bundled them into a spread of New Zealand finance companies and presented that as a risk-reducing strategy. Of course the entire finance company sector was fraught with specific risk: when it collapsed like a house of cards, it made little difference to the investor whether their portfolio comprised just one or five of the insolvent finance companies. They were toasted regardless. Strict control of the amount invested in any single issuer is paramount. We'll see in Chapters 8 and 9 just how rarely this basic rule has been followed by investment advisors in New Zealand.

2. Managing volatility (or market) risk

This is an altogether different concept to specific risk and is controlled by achieving a sufficient degree of diversification within a portfolio.

I'll talk more about diversification shortly, but the point is that while the price of assets moves up and down and some even go bust, your portfolio will always be subject to the general ups and downs of the market (this is what we call volatility) and you have to know how large a swing in overall value you can tolerate without losing sleep.

Once you limit the impact of specific risk (the effect from a specific security in your portfolio being wiped out) you're still left with volatility (the roller coaster of the ups and downs of portfolio value). It's the volatility of investment returns that makes the blending of the different asset classes (cash, fixed interest, shares and currency) in your portfolio so important. The blend can only be determined by the individual investor's particular tolerance for ups and downs.

Everyone has an appetite for returns on their investments; that's why we invest in the first place. But everyone is, to greater or lesser degrees, averse to volatility. It's a bit like spicy food; some like it hot, some like it mild, and for some, even the whiff of chilli or turmeric brings them out in a rash. Some people can tolerate the ups and downs of volatile markets. Some just can't — the sight of all those red arrows on the leader board brings on a panic attack.

An investor whose tolerance for month-to-month volatility is low will generally cope best with a portfolio that features more bonds and cash, while others are prepared to go on a bit of a roller-coaster ride, accepting it as the price they pay for higher returns over the long run. You can't, however, have one without the other!

So how do we structure a portfolio in order to match it to a client's tolerance for risk?

It's an exercise in spreading their funds across the various asset classes so as to meet their appetite for return/tolerance of volatility. And secondly to ensure that within each asset class the exposure to specific issuers is strictly capped so in the event that an issuer is wiped out, our investor is bruised rather than battered. Simple stuff really, which makes it so intriguing as to why New Zealand investment advisors, in the main, don't do it.

And how do we work out the risks inherent in each class of asset? This is the tricky bit, although history can help. The following summarises 86 years of history of the US market (we use the US market because it is the largest and has the longest history):

▷ Shares = 7.3 per cent average real return per annum with 30 per cent of years providing negative returns, the average annual loss being 15 per cent, the largest 40 per cent.

▷ Bonds = 1.0 per cent average real return per annum with 50 per cent of years providing negative returns, the average annual loss being 5 per cent, the largest 15 per cent.

▷ Cash = -0.5 per cent average real return per annum with 50 per cent of years providing negative returns, the average annual loss being 2.5 per cent, the largest being 15 per cent.

On the basis of history at least, the price of enjoying the significant returns after tax and inflation that a diversified share portfolio can provide is having to put up with a loss one year in three without freaking out if that loss is 15 per cent. That's just normal. Indeed, one in six loss years could destroy more than 30 per cent of your wealth.

At the other end of the volatility extreme is cash. But notice that after tax and inflation, historically you lose money — only 0.5 per cent per year, but you lose. Indeed, half the time you will lose, with the average loss year leaking away 2.5 per cent of your wealth.

Bonds sit in the middle, averaging a mere 1 per cent growth per annum, but again, they lose half the time, at a rate of about 5 per cent.

And remember these are the statistics for the last 86 years of market performance. It would be naïve to assume that such stats will typify your experience over, say, a 20-year period — which is what most people regard as 'an eternity' — let alone be a reliable guide to the next 20 years in particular.

In the next table, let's look at the last four 20-year periods and see what they tell us. Look at the column on shares. Sure, the long-term average might be 7.3 per cent, but in fact only one of the four 20-year periods has actually achieved this. And that's the point: if you invest on the basis that the long-term average returns will be reached over your

20-year period	Cash	Bonds	Shares
1929–48	-1.0%	1.2%	3.3%
1949–68	-0.2%	-1.0%	12.7%
1969–88	-1.1%	-0.4%	3.3%
1989–2008	0.0%	4.0%	6.1%
1994–2008	0.0%	3.6%	4.8%

'long term', you are likely to be disappointed — you may have several 20-year periods to wait! And even then, there are no guarantees. The table suggests you'd have better luck with bonds — the long-term, 1 per cent per annum average return has been reached over two of the four 20-year stretches. Heads, you win; tails, you lose.

And look at the last row, which shows what the last 15 years have been like. The margin of shares over bonds has hardly been the 7-to-1 long-term average!

Just to repeat: don't let anyone tell you that the long-term performance statistics of markets tell you anything reliable about even the next 10 or 20 years. Market performances are far too volatile for us to conclude that even the very long-term (100-year, say) averages tell us anything about the period we're concerned about (the next 20 years, say).

Let's illustrate the volatility/returns trade-off — or the conundrum that no saver can avoid.

The volatility/return trade-off

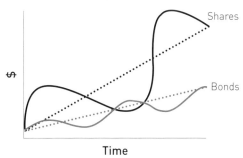

The graph on page 131 illustrates the price you must pay for growth. That price comes in the form of *volatility*, stylised by the wavy lines around the straight, dotted lines that denote the *trend* in the value of your investments. An investment in shares diversified by companies, sectors and countries will return more than one in the fixed interest of bonds. So the dotted or trend lines diverge over time. Now remember that 'over time' can mean a very long time, not just what seems like an eternity to you. If you bought shares at the first peak of the solid line that depicts their path in the graph, for example, you'd have to wait for close to two-thirds of the timeframe the graph covers before you even broke even. That can be 10 or more years — just to get your money back! You need, then, both to:

▷ accept that the value of your investment won't climb in a straight line but will more likely have ups and downs around that trend (as denoted above by the solid lines that waver around the respective trends); and
▷ accept that it's quite possible for a shares investment to drop even lower than one in fixed interest or bonds — that's how wavy (or volatile) share-investing can be.

Volatility, then, is a fact of life for investment portfolios. The relevant question is: How much volatility can you take? How much can your portfolio fall before you lose sleep, have a heart attack, knife your advisor, or jump from a high bridge? We all have different tolerances for volatility like this, and there is no way an advisor can construct a suitable portfolio for you without receiving from you a clear statement of how much volatility you're prepared to endure. None of us want volatility in our investment returns, but there's no investment on earth that doesn't give you a variable return — especially if you take inflation and currency fluctuations into account. In reality, then, we will all have portfolios that sit somewhere between the grey and black lines of the graph on the previous page — exactly where can only be determined by the specific answer to the volatility question.

Yet how many times do you hear the standard investment advice trotted about by so-called advisors — 'just stay in the market, eventually it will all come right'? A glance at the table on page 131 shows they have no basis on which to make that claim. It *might* come right. It might get worse. It might stay just as bad over the term you have available and then come right miraculously just after you've cashed out, because you couldn't stay in any longer. The only sensible approach to portfolio investment is to be flexible with respect to what proportion of your wealth you have invested in shares, bonds and cash and be prepared to shift those proportions around substantially in line with economic cycles, in order to pursue returns — always, of course, with due regard for preserving your wealth.

Now this is not the orthodoxy preached in the funds-management industry over recent decades. Rather, the consulting firms — for reasons that will become clear shortly — have perpetuated the myth that history is an infallible guide to the future, and that because shares have outperformed the other two asset classes over the long term, they must necessarily do so over the next relevant period. Oh, if only it were true! Investment life would be so simple — we'd just use all the statistical data from the past to work out what was going to happen in the future and design portfolios that provided optimal returns for risk for everybody — an easy-peasy, 'set-and-forget' strategy and the investors would all be so happy and prosperous.

And this is exactly what the consultant industry has done. It has taken the past as gospel, built statistical models based on that history and used them to convince well-meaning (but financially illiterate) trustees of superannuation and endowment funds to structure portfolios in line to these models. According to their advice, there is a fixed allocation range for each of cash, bonds and shares, and deferring to it is the most responsible way to manage money. Trustees — who in the main know little to nothing about portfolio theory or about economics, just want to 'do the right thing', and to avoid being pilloried for doing anything out of the ordinary — desperately seek someone they can cite as 'professional' to tell them what to do, so that if all turns to custard, they can plead that they were acting according to conventional wisdom. Meanwhile, even before all turns to custard, the funds just slowly but steadily leak value over time.

What a dream scenario for the multinational insurance industry conglomerates that own these consultant firms (yes, we'll talk about that conflict of interest later) — clients who are so conservative, so incapable of making the decisions themselves and so ready to follow the 'respectable' course that you could lead them all over a cliff, so long as everyone else was travelling that way. And that's exactly what's happened in the funds-management business internationally over the last 30 years. There have been legions of well-meaning but financially illiterate folk put in charge of large dollops of funds, who have all been only too willing for the large portfolio consultant businesses to lead them, by the nose, to oblivion.

It's reminiscent of the carnage the banks have just caused with their charge into the derivatives markets, subscribing to products so complex that the issuers don't understand them, let alone the poor old purchaser. There seems to be an inevitability about human behaviour — following *en masse* the latest fad no matter how irrational, how unsustainable, and how self-destructive it might be. The funds-management industry is a prime example of this compulsive, masochistic tendency.

Herds will always gather, work themselves into a frenzy over some new opportunity, over-invest on the back of extreme positivism, and run over a cliff as a result. The fact is that markets are simply the places where humans can express their exuberance, their anxieties, their hopes, their woes — and along the way flog each other into frenzied extremes of each. The key to outperforming that norm on a sustained and long-term basis is to see this behaviour for what it is. Irrespective of what the crowd and its motivators thinks assess, every time you make an investment decision, what the crowd is doing.

The past — even the long-term past — is a lousy indicator of the future, but it doesn't follow that all investment must necessarily be blind. There's much to learn from the madness of crowds, the pace of market momentum, the trends within the economy at any time. It's distilling this — discovering the relationships between the underlying logic of markets and the behaviour of investors — that makes for astute, logically coherent and defensible investment decisions. And you wonder why insurance salesmen posing as investment advisors don't do too well?

Beyond the noise of fads and crowd behaviour, there are certain fundamental principles. In growing economies, the value of real assets should lift, and if an asset reaps a higher and higher income over time, then it should be worth more as time goes by. But boy do we know that valuations of assets go all over the park on the road to the future! So yes, it's an article of faith that share values — which are the claims on these productive assets — will rise over time in line with the higher income a prospering, growing economy generates.

So if it's preserving wealth that's the main objective with a personal savings portfolio — enhancing it as much as possible, of course, but subject to your intolerance of losing it — then own some shares by all means. But don't fall for this dumber-than-dumb line peddled by brokers, fund managers and the soft-shoe salespeople posing as financial advisors that shares will always do better.

3. Dynamic diversification

There's more to achieving effective diversification than you might at first think.

Maintaining effective diversification is a dynamic game. Any advisor or fund manager has a real obligation to maintain the diversification that you need in your portfolio. He or she can do this by spreading the portfolio across lots of different securities, each picked on merit; however, it must be remembered that it is a dynamic, not a 'set-and-forget' process. One set of economic circumstances, for instance, can mean that shares and bonds will behave differently and hence provide you with effective diversification if you're spread across them; but a different set of circumstances may well eliminate the value of any diversification between stocks and bonds.

We've just seen an instance (the 2008 credit crunch) where corporate bonds and shares behaved in the same manner: everything tanked. Diversification across the two asset classes didn't mitigate the risk after all. Anyone who was economically literate should have seen *that* coming. The credit crunch arose because of widespread concern over whether banks and other businesses could honour their liabilities — whether they would issue shares or bonds to their creditors. We correspondingly (and predictably) saw a sell-off in both asset classes. This was as loud a signal to adjust asset allocation and flee to cash as a market could ever give.

They don't even teach this stuff in investment management courses, so many of the advisors and fund managers holding diplomas from such polytechnics — not to mention other, even less impressive, private-industry fill-out-the-form certificates — haven't a clue about this reality. In other words, when it comes to economics, they're totally illiterate — and yet you let them manage your money. From 2007 to 2009, advisors or fund managers that kept your money in just two asset classes (shares and bonds) — presumably reassuring themselves that one or the other might be at risk, but they were diversified against it — took a pounding. We saw in Chapter 5 that such a static approach is exactly what the Cullen Fund did. It held only 5 per cent of its funds in cash throughout the financial-sector meltdown. It's a stunning example of investment management inertia, and the scale of its losses demonstrates that.

Retail investors suffered similar wealth destruction through lack of dynamism. Given that most managers lacked the foresight and the ability to move outside rigid benchmark constrictions, it was pretty much a sure thing you'd be toast, and have to swallow 'returns' of minus 20 to 40 per cent, in some cases, more. If you nail your colours to the mast of the market benchmark (the 'set-and-forget' approach), then you have to accept whatever the climate or conditions throw at you. And if the market founders seriously, it's Davey Jones' Locker for you too, me hearty. It just doesn't make sense, and the results show that.

The idea, then, that you can determine an investor's tolerance for volatility, set their asset allocation between, say, shares, cash, government bonds and corporate bonds — and then just leave the asset allocation to look after itself — is the most telling indicator of investment illiteracy on the part of the very many advisors and fund managers who do exactly that.

But it is not correct to conclude from the fact that most investors (including professionals) don't even make market-average returns that it's impossible to do so. Instead, it should serve as a warning. Mediocrity is widespread, but it's not industry-wide.

4. Home bias

Currency volatility dictates that you must spread your assets globally. Most Kiwis maintain a grossly overweight financial exposure to New Zealand. It's typical of what we call 'home-country bias', and we're not unique in that regard. It's not only that we tend to hold New Zealand shares and New Zealand fixed interest and don't step too much outside this, but it's also that we have a large exposure to begin with in the shape of our house and our job. So for most of us, it makes sense to funnel funds offshore. That won't always be the case: for example, a retired investor seeking high and predictable cash drawings from their portfolio will need much of their portfolio retained in their home currency and in low-volatility asset types.

The folly of home bias is easy to demonstrate. What matters when you cash in an investment for the purposes of spending the proceeds is the price of what you're buying — not what currency that price is denominated in. More specifically, what matters is what determines the price of whatever it is you want to spend your money on. Increasingly in a deregulated market, it is global competitive pressures that determine prices — quite independent of any New Zealand factors. The price of the car or LCD television you buy, or the overseas trip you take, is increasingly driven by global, not local, forces. It's even more internationalised than that, in fact — the cost of a haircut is determined by the value of the currency it's priced in, so as the New Zealand dollar falls, the cost of a haircut falls if you've stored your funds beyond New Zealand.

So you have to maximise your wealth in a way that gives you the most to buy global products. This means going for an investment portfolio to maximise your wealth in 'global dollars' — that mix of currencies that reflects where you source the basket of goods and services you purchase. And maximising wealth in 'global dollars' requires a global spread of assets — even if you just have cash, you need to spread it around and towards those currencies with the strongest prospects.

The case for owning predominantly New Zealand assets in a portfolio is very weak indeed. This applies equally to fixed interest as it does to shares — to minimise your exchange rate risk on your fixed- interest portfolio you should also spread it around. You might measure your New Zealand assets against a New Zealand dollar benchmark and conclude that all is well; but that can be a smokescreen if the New Zealand dollar has fallen from US80c to US50c in the meantime.

There's no escaping that you need a global portfolio, so you also need to contain your exposure to New Zealand within prudent limits. For almost all New Zealanders, that currently means redistributing assets from the domestic economy to the global one.

5. Inflation

This isn't something we've had to think an awful lot about for most of the past 25 years. If you're Generation X or younger it's going to be well outside your experience. But don't think it can't happen again — because it can — and eventually, once the world has dug itself out of the mess that the 2008 credit crunch exposed, a spell of strong inflation is virtually guaranteed. And if you have all your money sitting at the bank, earning not much interest, woe betide ye! If inflation takes off, you'll have lost your purchasing power, big time. So the effect of inflation needs to be factored into the mix of what assets to have in your investment portfolio.

Inflation can erode the value of your portfolio very quickly. Just ask all those savers who had bank deposits back in the early '70s. Inflation will return, if not tomorrow, then the day after tomorrow. We don't know exactly when, but the ground is being prepared, with all the economic stimulus measures (all that trillion-dollar spending) that governments are deploying to address the current crisis. Inflation at 15 per cent, interest rates at 5 per cent (before tax!) and you're under-water before you know it. So best be prepared and make sure you've got some inflation-hedging assets (growth assets such as equities, commodities, maybe inflation-linked bonds) in your toolbox.

6. Tax

Just a short one, this, but remember that tax sees to it that the playing field ain't ever level. It's all very well to be continually seeking out assets that have patterns of return that are not completely correlated to one another, but that whole pursuit of dynamic asset allocation can be terribly frustrated by the advent of new tax rules. Currently in New Zealand, for example, we have a bizarre situation for wealth-preserving investors whereby two quite different tax regimes apply depending on whether we're talking about the Australasian stocks held in your portfolio or stocks from any other part of the world. In short, you're taxed on the proceeds when you sell Australasian shares, which means a strategy of 'dynamic portfolio management' — altering your holdings according to market conditions and, inevitably, buying and selling holdings — is disadvantageous from the perspective of tax efficiency. Buying and selling shares in companies beyond Australasia, by contrast, escapes the dead eye of the taxman, so dynamic adjustment of portfolios is fine. The predictable consequence is that there's a loss of portfolio investment interest in Australasia by Kiwis.

The message is simple: before implementing a portfolio investment strategy, sort out what the implications of the tax regime are.

8

Seeking professional help — but getting stitched up

If, like many New Zealanders, you have trouble telling the difference between shares and bonds, don't know how to take a short position, let alone a long one, get confused by talk of leveraging and wouldn't know a collateralised debt obligation if you got bitten by one — and plenty of people have been bitten by them just lately — who you gonna call?

The traditional sources of investment advice are numerous, ranging from the private banking divisions of the large banks, boutique investment houses, sharebrokers, chains of investment advisors (most owned by insurance companies), to independent investment advisors or financial-planning bucket shops squeezed in between the fish-and-chip and burger bars of Main Street New Zealand. Each of these has a different heritage, has entered the advisory business for different reasons, and brings with it a unique set of skills in practising their financial alchemy upon the investing public.

There's plenty of good investment advice out there, and some astute, dedicated, honest and competent advisors, who are prepared to ignore the hype that's just about as thick on the ground at the wholesale level as it is at the retail, and do their own research. But it's doubtful whether the goodies outnumber the sum total of the incompetent, the charlatans and the downright crooks, who have been allowed to proliferate by woefully inadequate regulation.

In this chapter, we have a look at some of the more common deficiencies and malpractices rife in the financial advisory sector, with reference to some case studies. Like most horror-show rides in Halloween theme parks, we'll start with the merely frightful and save the real shockers for last.

Sharebrokers

Investment is a highly personal thing, largely dependent on your personality, your tolerance for risk, your appetite for reward and, of course, your hopes, aspirations, your time of life and your means. So financial advice should be largely bespoke — made to order, and made to fit.

The acid test, then, of how suitable someone presenting themselves to you as your advisor actually is, has to be whether he or she is an 'advisor' in the true sense of the word — whether they act for you and you alone on portfolio matters. After all, you go to a doctor and you expect him to be addressing your health rather than looking for excuses to peddle the products of the drug companies for the commission they'll send his way. Oops! Bad example!

A sharebroker certainly isn't a disinterested advisor whom you hire to give independent advice based purely and solely on your individual interests and pay them directly for that advice. But at least they're upfront about it: the word 'broker' in their name describes the relationship. They're in the business of selling you shares (and usually, bonds, futures and other securities) for the commission they receive on each sale. Happily, since they're also in a competitive industry, they'll mostly do their best to ensure they sell you winners, as a sharebroking firm that has a reputation for picking winners will attract greater market share. But in terms of investment advice broadly conceived, their usefulness to you as an advisor is limited. This is because of their approach to investment strategy, costs, reporting, proactivity, diversification, and independence.

Investment strategy from a sharebroker tends to be 'bottom-up' —

selecting the hottest stock and adding it to your portfolio so that, over time, you can end up with an almost random mix of stock picks with no coherent, underpinning strategy. This reflects the heritage of the sharebroking industry. It is traditionally based on individual company research, stock-picking advice and the promotion of new issues for individual companies.

Costs can be very high — brokerage can be 2 per cent or more per deal if outside New Zealand and Australia. There can be minimum transaction costs for US shares of US$150 per trade; you need big investments to make such trades cost-effective. For this reason, broker portfolios are often concentrated mainly in New Zealand and Australian stocks and lack *diversification* as a result. Ultimately, over-exposure to this small part of the world will confirm it's not a sound, long-term wealth-preservation strategy. What's more, you'll be hit with high 'custody fees' from a broker. Surrendering custody of your scrip (the titles to the securities you own) is important for transactions on your portfolio to be able to be conducted quickly and efficiently, but you do become reliant on the integrity of the custody reporting system and the security of the funds, so ensuring that you're getting adequate safekeeping is an important element of this decision.

There are other dangers too. The investor bears *additional costs* when they're being advised to take an entitlement in an issue of new shares or bonds in which the sharebroker is the lead manager, and is paid a commission by the issuer from the launch premium.

And frequently, the type of securities you'll be landed with by a sharebroker will be illiquid, limiting how much practical adjustment the broker can perform on your portfolio. This can become a spiral of neglect. Without being periodically updated, the value of a portfolio can suffer. As its value declines, so too will the broker's inclination to look at it again. 'Set-and-forget' can set in. We see this lack of *proactivity* in portfolios that come across our desk all the time. Many haven't been adjusted for years. The periodic meetings you might have with your broker, who pats your hand and mouths a few platitudes, might be superficially reassuring, and reminding them you exist may land you the odd entitlement in a new issue or similar, but the reality is you're unlikely to get quality portfolio management from a sharebroker.

And worst of all, because they rely on commissions or brokerage for their remuneration, I believe there's the inevitable temptation to channel clients into those areas where the rewards are highest for the broker, regardless of how appropriate they are for the client's portfolio. It takes a very strong broker indeed to avoid this moral hazard and evidence of their failure to overcome the temptation shows up in portfolios patently overweight in stocks in which their broker distributed the float (the IPO, or initial public offer). The lack of *diversification* is certainly not in the client's interest. The 2008 portfolio on the next page, constructed by a major sharebroker, illustrates this.

The fixed interest is weighted towards paper that the broker brought to market and towards issuers who paid high commissions to those placing their stock (such as finance companies, who must use fat commissions to overpower brokers' wariness and resistance to their low credit ratings). As a result, this portfolio is underweight in high-quality bonds such as senior bank debt, which would have protected this client against the market downturn. After all, the point of the fixed-interest end of the portfolio is to provide ballast to the sail of the high-flying (and hard-falling) shares and property assets. When the fixed interest you're carrying is also risky, you'll find yourself seriously over-canvassed in inclement weather. Next, issues underwritten directly by the broker comprise 13 per cent of the portfolio.

What we see is a hotchpotch of securities that appear to owe their presence more to their role as sources of commissions and brokerage for the advisor than to any concept of the quality and diversification that is in the client's interest. Global Corporate Credit Notes, Strategic Finance, Babcock and Brown and Credit Sail have all failed, so it's a bad portfolio anyway, just on the grounds of how much of each of those the client owns. Many of the other holdings have suffered capital erosion, too, with the effect that this investor, who requested a 'low-risk' portfolio, has lost 25 per cent or more of its value. Better to have left the money in the bank.

Broker 1

Description	Status	Percentage of portfolio
Cash		6%
Fixed interest		68%
Equities Two listed shares		12%
Property Three listed property companies including Kermadec		14%
Total		100%

How can we not conclude that the opportunity for the advisor to obtain commission income or brokerage was the reason for inappropriate diversification? It certainly cannot be argued this portfolio was in any way optimal for the investor.

Another 2008 portfolio constructed by a leading local broker looked okay at a glance — lots of equities representing exposure to a range of sectors, and a healthy lack of sick finance companies. So congratulations on that. But when I took a more critical eye, bearing in mind the principles of sound portfolio construction from the previous chapter, there was a glaring lack of diversification beyond New Zealand and Australia; unfortunately this is a very common theme for the broker portfolios that cross our desks. It was also over concentrated upon single issuers, lacked currency diversification, and showed little evidence of any strategy to exit poorly performing sectors (finance and property) or to adjust asset allocation in favour of global cash. The overall liquidity of the fixed-interest portion of the portfolio was poor, ensuring that in a sinking market the ability to exit wasn't there.

And, again, it looked to me as though commission income seemed to have had an undue influence over security selection. For brokers, commissions from newly issued securities or underwriting fees are core income; no fewer than eight of the securities in the portfolio were ones where the broker was joint or lead manager of the offer. The question has to be asked — shouldn't a conflict of interest exclude the broker from advising clients to buy such securities?

The equities portion was virtually all a range of New Zealand and Australian stock-picks. With only 20 per cent of the portfolio outside New Zealand, the portfolio represented a high-risk bet on the Australasian economy — with only one lonely international hedging bet — Guinness Peat Group!

Investment advisors and financial planners

There are hundreds of these, but on any objective analysis, few could call themselves 'independent' or use the word 'advisor' in anything approaching its true meaning. That's a bone of contention I have had with the regulators in New Zealand for years now, and they still haven't acted to protect the public. It's not just an abuse of the English language that's at stake: it leads people innocently to believe that these service providers act in the interest of their clients, or are independent of insurance companies and other product pushers. In the UK, this has been a huge issue and there's been some decisive curtailing of the abuse of the words 'independent' and 'advisor'. Our regulator snores.

Many so-called 'independent advisors' in New Zealand are simply commission salesmen who get their income from recommending products that pay high commissions. It's clear that financial advisors have little market knowledge or qualifications or, most relevantly, physical investment experience. You can get something called a Postgraduate Diploma in Financial Planning to help you make the transition from selling used cars or real estate into a similar gig in finance: most polytechs will fit you out with one, or you might find one in your box of cornies, for all they're worth.

The diploma doesn't teach investment prowess, and holding one doesn't automatically confer it, either. That can only come from investment market experience and/or strong tertiary qualifications in investment theory and economics. But in general, people graduating with those tend to practise as analysts or economists rather than share their expertise directly with the public. The public, sadly, is left to deal with salesmen who pretend they are advisors — and worse, who are scandalously allowed to do this.

The relevant industry associations perpetuate the myth that somehow these salespeople are 'independent'. Yet some members of both the IFA (Institute of Financial Advisers) or SIFA (Society of *Independent* Financial Advisers), my italics, are anything but independent, as they merrily receive commissions from product providers — indeed, the level of commissions they receive from product sellers is often indexed to how much of that provider's product they sell! Their conferences (sponsored by the providers, of course) feature trade displays of providers' product ranges and, in general, having a browse around the stalls is about as hard as it gets for these salesmen as they try to choose what to fit their clients out with.

Now, there's a logical link between high commissions and high-risk products. If your here-today/gone-tomorrow finance company has failed to qualify for any kind of decent credit rating, it'll need to think of some stunt to attract business. Greasing the palms of 'independent' financial advisors' with higher-than-normal commissions is a good place to start, and so often these overcome any queasiness advisors may fleetingly feel.

It's the dominance of the space by product providers and commissions that has led to the portfolios constructed by New Zealand financial advisors ending up so laced with toxic products from finance companies, as well as big-commission products such as Liontamer, OM-IP, ING and bank retail unit trusts. MFS (the precursor to Vestar) and Strategic Finance were regular sponsors of industry conferences, splashing out generously on lavish dinners and glitzy venues to dazzle commission-hungry 'independent' advisors and help them feel good about their products. What a pity neither shop invested more in protecting the interests of the members of the public who would end up fitted out with their toxic products. The sheer inability of some New Zealand financial advisors to look beyond the jing-a-ling being dangled in front of their noses by sponsors, and look at their real quality (or lack of it), is the single best reason they should be disqualified from the privilege of looking after the public's money. The blind faith placed by so-called trained, 'independent' financial advisors in certain managers, based on little more than a free lunch, lavish conference, or a trip to Fiji, has led directly to a significant proportion of the savings of retail investors being concentrated in a narrow range of toxic products, heedless (supposing the 'trained advisors' were ever aware of the concept) of the desirability of diversification. Too many advisors have turned out to be little more than financial planning prostitutes controlled by commission-wielding provider pimps.

Often houses aggregate to form a chain of advisors that have an imposing market presence and generate a national brand — Spicers, Money Managers and Vestar are examples. This is based on the well-known marketing principle that the bigger a brand, the greater the trust the public generally place in it (illogical though this can be). It's worked — never mind that the insertion of head office structures into these organisations has done little but add overheads and, of course, amplify the national marketing presence. Certainly the standard of financial advice doesn't necessarily improve, as the cases show.

1. Spicers

Let's look first at Spicers. With their numerous offices and veritable herd of advisors, they're a great example of a high-cost advisory service. These reporting costs and custody costs all have to be covered by the client, as well as the fees to mother — these days Spicers is owned by the French insurance giant AXA. Needless to say, AXA isn't in it for love despite its French pedigree, and now that they've swallowed up the recently-defunct advisory chain of Vestar, the overhead they impose can only have grown. Their stable of advisors has grown to 60 in 25 locations — all for a mere $1.5 billion under management. That is a massive overhead — little wonder the advisors push a plethora of in-house unit trusts and related-party funds; the income generated

Spicers portfolio 2008

Description	Percentage of portfolio
Income assets	
New Zealand Bonds	
AMP Capital Investors	4%
ING (New Zealand) Limited	2%
New Zealand Income	
Arcus Investment Management	11%
Offshore bonds	
Arcus Investment Management	3%
PIMCO/Blackrock	24%
Growth assets	
Australasian companies	
Alliance Bernstein	5%
Brook Asset Management	5%
Milford Asset Management	3%
MIR Investment Management	3%
Offshore companies	
Bernstein Value Equities	5%
Capital International / LSV / GMO	17%
Legg Mason	4%
RCM	6%
Property & infrastructure	
Brook Asset Management	3%
LaSalle / CBRE	3%
Mint Asset Management	2%
Total	100%

from these is all needed to help support this behemoth.

The larger advisory shops thrive on the layercake of fees they impose. They must now disclose these, but all that's required is a pretty vague sort of disclosure, and the information can be scattered throughout the Investment Statement — often 30 pages or more of pure, impenetrable legalese — so getting to the good oil is about as likely for the reader as a successful treasure hunt.

Mr and Mrs XYZ had money invested with Spicers in the 'moderate portfolio'. Their funds were placed in a single unit trust that was then spread across a series of other unit trusts — a classic 'fund-of-funds' model, where the investor hasn't got a hope in hell of working out how much of which individual securities ultimately comprise their portfolio. At best, they get thrown a few scraps of information on the 'major' holdings.

The fees charged on the total suite of portfolio management were horrendous and somewhat disguised. While the 'portfolio service fee' seemed cheap — approximately 0.3 per cent per annum — the fees charged within the single unit trust into which the funds were placed were close to 2.08 per cent. That's a management fee of approximately 2.38 per cent per annum of your portfolio. In other words, if you had $1 million invested, the Spicers fee is around $24,000 per annum. Fees of around half that are commonplace. It would take a stellar performance by the fund to provide a meaningful return once the fees and the various tax inefficiencies incurred along the way were deducted — pity that stellar performance wasn't forthcoming.

Not that you'd really know, of course, because all those fees you were forking out didn't quite run to buying you transparency. You would have to wade through the quarterly reports of how each individual investment in the 'moderate portfolio' performed. Then you could assemble all that disparate information into a table like the one on page 148 to show you what your holdings were.

And then you could look at the performance. Offshore companies comprise a third of the portfolio and the return for the year ending 30 September 2008 on that sector was negative 24.5 per cent versus an MSCI (world share market index return) of negative 17.7 per cent. Clearly the offshore manager selection has been poor. But anyone can have a bum year; let's look at the performance over the last five years. The offshore companies' return over that period has been 3.3 per cent per annum, compared to 4.9 per cent per annum for the index, and that's before tax.

So how did the fixed-interest end of the portfolio get on? Over the year, Spicers' New Zealand bonds portfolio was up 5.4 per cent (before tax) versus a 50/50 government bond and 90-day bank bill index of 9.4 per cent. Over five years, that number is 4.3 per cent per annum against the index return of 6.4 per cent per annum.

So you're forking out nearly $24,000 per annum for what exactly? There's no evidence of performance value-add here whatsoever — none. There's certainly no assurance that all those fees will even keep your returns up with the indexes of market-average performance.

2. Vestar

Spicers isn't unusual — the financial advisory sector in New Zealand is just riddled with examples of the toxic mix of high fees and poor portfolio structures. The following is a portfolio for a client of the late Vestar chain that (as noted above) has now been swallowed up by AXA. This client specified a 'conservative' risk profile, and what they got is shown opposite.

Today, this portfolio has less than 20 per cent liquidity (that is, the client may physically draw down only 20 per cent of their portfolio), with the balance locked up in defaulted finance companies and property companies and with very little prospect of seeing much of it back. So much for conservative!

Fixed-interest instruments tend to be conservative options — unless the fixed-interest return they offer is nothing more than the number some shady finance company executive promises you, his fingers firmly crossed behind his back as he fervently hopes everyone on his loan book can keep up their payments on their used, imported Nissan Cedrics. We see 10 fixed-interest instruments in this portfolio, but every single one of them has been frozen or gone under. Just holding 10 junk bonds doesn't equate to diversification — it's actually a single, ill-advised bet on junk bonds!

The property sector of the portfolio comprises unlisted and very illiquid property syndicates. There's no way now for investors to get their money out unless they find some poor sucker to buy their shares, because the funds' liquidity has been crippled by people who were smart and informed enough to get out while they could — smarter and better informed than our trained professional from Vestar, at any rate.

Vestar 2008 and supposed to be a conservative portfolio

Description	Status	Percentage of portfolio
Cash		
AUD call account		5%
NZD call account		4%
Fixed interest		
Cymbis Finance Ltd	Receivership	4%
ING Diversified Yield Fund	Frozen	5%
OPI Pacific Finance Ltd	Liquidation	6%
Boston Finance Ltd	Moratorium	9%
Bridgecorp Ltd	Receivership	3%
Capital and Merchant Finance Ltd	Receivership	9%
IMP Diversified Income Fund Ltd	Moratorium	8%
OPI Pacific Finance Ltd (30-day term deposit)	Liquidation	7%
OPI Pacific Finance Ltd (Secured debenture stock)	Liquidation	9%
PropertyFinance Securities Ltd	Receivership	8%
Property		
Clendon Shopping Centre	Illiquid	5%
MINT Australia NZ Real Estate Investment Trust		6%
Radius Properties Ltd	Illiquid	7%
St Laurence Property Development Fund	Illiquid	5%
Total		100%

Who knows what the value of these assets is? There's simply no market for them. Such share values as there are for Radius and Clendon are guesses based on some presumed asset backing, but the fact that the more liquid listed property shares have been trading well below *their* asset-backing indicates that the reported valuations are fantasy.

So how did our client, who requested a 'conservative' investment strategy from the trained expert from Vestar, end up standing amid the rubble of their hard-earned savings? Well, it's hard not to conclude that the advisor was out there chasing commissions to the exclusion of all other considerations. The real giveaway is the reeking basket of fixed-interest instruments. Out of the entire constellation of fixed-interest instruments out there, how did our client end up with 10 of the very dodgiest? Bad luck, or could it have anything to do with the fact that all 10 were paying fat commissions in return for the business? The charming folk at Vestar — now moved on to similar houses still operating — know the answers.

3. Imperial Investments

A lesser-known 'independent' is Imperial Investments Ltd. Their website states:

> Taking advantage of market psychology and price actions impacted by accumulation and distribution in the market allows the firm to achieve positive results in both up and down cycles in the market.

Imperial Investments Limited 2007

Description	Status	Percentage of portfolio
GIS Conservative Growth		20%
GIS Super Yield Fund	Frozen	24%
ING Regular Income Fund	Frozen	28%
TSB term deposit		20%
ASB term deposit		5%
St Laurence debentures	Moratorium	3%
Total		100%

Hell! Sounds like magic! What's their secret?

Well, first you construct a portfolio, like the one shown above. And, hey presto!

Oops.

Imperial have managed to erode this client's capital by 55 per cent. It's a bit like the magic trick where the magician saws the lady in half, except unlike in the magic trick, you end up only getting half the lady back. That's what happens when you never so much as attempt to balance the high-risk yield and income funds you've plunged your clients' hard-won savings into.

4. Investor Link

Investor Link in Christchurch constructed the little beauty opposite for a client in their late sixties. The mandate when you're looking at all that grey hair across your desk is, of course, that you should be putting them into more conservative assets or risk-reducing assets. And even if they express a bit of a tolerance for risk, because the market's buoyant, say, you should be keeping a weather eye out for a downturn so that you can shift their holdings into cash. After all, the last thing a couple nearing the end of their working and earning lives wants is to have to rebuild their wealth due to market-related shocks.

On paper, this portfolio appears to be well diversified across a broad range of markets and includes some listed shares and listed trusts (the significance of these is that the advisor has resisted the temptation to cop out on picking securities themselves and instead ploughed their client into managed funds, which come with yet another layer of fees). The advisor has also been bold enough (not all are) to steer some of the money into OM-IPs, (which are 'an alternative investment' from Australian issuer Man Investments) and the portfolio has been rewarded accordingly, as many of the OM-IP products have more than justified the fees and commissions paid to the advisor.

But setting aside quibbling about what bets paid off and what didn't, far and away the worst aspect of this portfolio is the *type* of portfolio it is, considering the people it's for. It's allocated nearly 70 per cent towards growth assets with only 30 per cent in the cash, fixed interest and income assets. Based on the age and stage of this couple the mix should be the other way round. Wasn't that printed on the cornies packet that the 'advisor's' diploma came in?

And faced with the impending global crisis, Investor Link proved

Investor Link 2008

Description	Status	Percentage of portfolio
Cash & fixed interest		
AUD		1%
NZD		2%
Liontamer Money series1		2%
Liontamer Money series3		2%
PM Capital Enhanced Yield		5%
Canterbury Mortgage Trust	Frozen	3%
Dorchester	Moratorium	3%
Provincial	Receivership	1%
South Canterbury		5%
Challenger Professional	Temporarily closed	1%
LM First Mortgage	Closed lack of liquidity	3%
Equities		
BHP		3%
JBWere Emerging Leaders		2%
Telstra Warrants		1%
Blackrock Mining		1%
BT Wholesale		2%
Ecofin Water & Power		2%
Foreign & Colonial		3%
Liontamer Fallen Angel		2%
Liontamer Tiger series 3		3%
Platinum International		11%
RIT Capital		6%
SVG		1%
Alternative		
Liontamer Combi series3		2%
Liontamer Combi series5		2%
OM-IP 140 (AUD)		3%
OM-IP 140 (NZD)		4%
OM-IP 220 series12		3%
OM-IP 220 series4		10%
OM-IP 220 series6		9%
OM-IP hedge plus		2%
Total		100%

to be a possum in the headlights. What's wrong with cash, cash, and more cash when everything else is melting down?

Fully 11 per cent of this portfolio is frozen in impaired assets, i.e. Provincial (note that this has been written down in the portfolio to value it as at 23 December 2008), Dorchester, Canterbury Mortgage Trust and then the likes of the illiquid Challenger Professional High Yield Fund. On the Challenger website, they state in regards to the Challenger Professional High Yield Fund: 'On 16 October 2008, the withdrawal process for the Fund was amended. As a result, you will only be able to withdraw from the Fund if we make an offer of withdrawal.'

So what was Investor Link doing *before* 16 October 2008, when everyone else who was in the know was beating down Challenger's door to get their money out? Either they didn't see it coming, or they just didn't give a toss; either way, it's not a good look.

And why is 43 per cent of this couple's portfolio crammed with funds such as the OM-IPs and the Liontamers, unless it has something to do with the high commissions they are paying?

5. Muriel Dunn

Muriel Dunn is a larger-than-life lady with a personality as big as Texas. Her practice in Hamilton was large and attracted many of that city's most vulnerable. She recently sold her business for the princely sum of one single dollar and retained all the liabilities. She's now the subject of legal proceedings from her shattered and disgruntled client base. This portfolio was apportioned as shown in the table on page 156.

How is this portfolio flawed? Let me count the ways! It lacks any attempt at effective diversification. It features a large number of fixed-interest instruments, most of which, sadly, are from finance companies and therefore amount to a single bad gamble on that sector. These were presumably supposed to balance the 'risky' end of the portfolio, the handful of equities — most from within New Zealand — and the single, low-quality property trust. With this portfolio, 10 of the 16 fixed-interest assets, equating to 65 per cent of the portfolio, are in various stages of illiquidity, moratorium, deep freeze or bankruptcy,

Muriel Dunn Financial Services 2007

Description	Status	Percentage of portfolio
Marac on-call		5%
Macquarie GEA account		2%
Fixed interest/bonds		
Bastion Finance Ltd		4%
BridgeCorp Secured Debenture Stock	Receivership	6%
Dominion Finance Debenture Stock	Receivership	9%
Five Star Consumer Finance	Receivership	6%
Hanover Finance Ltd	Moratorium	16%
MSF Pacific Finance	Liquidation	10%
North South Finance Ltd	Moratorium	4%
St Laurence Ltd	Moratorium	11%
United Finance Ltd	Moratorium	3%
Transpower NZ bonds		4%
Hamilton City Council		2%
South Canterbury Finance		3%
Allied Prime Finance Ltd		1%
Equities		
Fisher Funds NZ Growth Fund		2%
Auckland International Airport		2%
Grange Resources Ltd		2%
Telecom Corporation NZ		1%
Westpac Banking Corporation		2%
Property		
ING Property Trust		5%
Total		100%

and with the New Zealand share market in disarray (taking all of the holdings in this portfolio with it), there's hardly anything left.

There has to have been a serious conflict of interest, as these companies have dished out commission to Muriel in order for her to raise capital from the unsuspecting public. What, you may ask (and someone has to, because the regulator clearly hasn't) gives this woman the right to dress herself up as a reputable 'financial planner'?

When the Hanover Finance investment matured, Muriel Dunn Financial Services wrote to the client explaining that the bet on Hanover could be renewed, but since that one issue represented more than 16 per cent of the portfolio, she recommended the client consider splitting this into two parcels 'to meet the criteria of the Investment Placement Committee'. She recommended half the funds be placed into Hanover for 24 months at 8.85 per cent and the other half into Belgrave Finance Limited for 18 months at 10.20 per cent. I guess the extra 1.35 per cent interest that Belgrave was offering reflected the added risk factor, as it was placed into receivership within 12 months of the recommendation, even as the rumours around Hanover got louder.

Muriel Dunn is like many financial planners — a great people person, a motivator, a hugely personable woman who could help you through that relationship break-up or guide that colour choice for your walls. You'd go to her any day if you wanted help to give up smoking. But as a financial planner, I reckon the lady was a tramp.

6. Alison Renfrew of Lyford Asset Management

Next, let's have a look at the work of Richard and Alison Renfrew, not only certified financial planners ('the pinnacle of achievement in the industry', as their website puts it), but Alison was also Certified Financial Planner of the Year for 2004 (presumably the pinnacle of the pinnacle). The portfolio Lyford Asset Management Ltd put together is shown on page 158.

The Renfrews' portfolio advice was hugely flawed.

In the portfolio, Bridgecorp made up 12 per cent of the total investment. Well, plenty of people were gullible enough to invest in Bridgecorp, including quite a few financial planners and advisors. But what were they doing rolling over these monies in May 2007, only two months before Bridgecorp itself rolled over? It's not as though you could ignore the warnings that were rife in light of how deep the poo that Bridgecorp's Australian arm was in at that time.

Did Renfrew, or Lyfords, 'independently research' the financials of Bridgecorp, and talk to the directors or the CEO to make up their own mind about the health of the company? I hope that the lucrative upfront commissions on offer if they sent business Bridgecorp's way didn't render all such questions irrelevant.

A piece in the *Sunday Star-Times* by a chap with the exquisitely appropriate name of Rob Stock revealed that Bridgecorp were paying unusually high commissions of up to 3 per cent.[1] How can any advisor look you in the eye and claim they're 'independent' when they're consigning you to almost certain oblivion at the hands of a company founded by a person previously known for losing investors millions and that, for good measure, was known at the time to be again in severe financial strife, all for the sake of the commission? The very best thing they could claim in their defence is that they are incompetent. Either

Lyfords 2008

Description	Status	Percentage of portfolio
Cash & fixed interest		
Bank deposits		25%
Bridgecorp - rolled 20/07/2006	Receivership	3%
Bridgecorp - rolled 2/05/2007	Receivership	7%
Bridgecorp - rolled 21/05/2007	Receivership	2%
PPS International fixed interest Fund		5%
Equities		
PPS Australasian Equities Fund		6%
PPS NZ Equities Fund		7%
PPS International Equities Fund		12%
Property		
PPS Property Fund		4%
Other assets		
PPS Platinum International Fund		10%
PPS Mortgage Fund		6%
PPS Balanced Fund		10%
Liontamer		3%
Total		100%

Lyfords 2007

Description	Status	Percentage of portfolio
Cash & fixed interest		
PPS International fixed interest Fund		44%
PPS NZ fixed interest Fund		7%
Equity		
PPS Asia Fund		3%
PPS Australasian Equities Fund		6%
PPS NZ Equities Fund		6%
PPS International Equities Fund		20%
PPS Platinum International Fund		6%
Property		
PPS Property Fund		4%
Alternative assets		
PPS Diversified Trading Fund	Closed	4%
Total		100%

Lyfords 2007

Description	Status	Percentage of portfolio
Cash & fixed interest		
AUD		1%
GBP		0%
NZD		1%
ING Credit Opportunities	Suspended	4%
ING Regular Income	Frozen	8%
Bridgecorp	Receivership	3%
Bridgecorp	Receivership	2%
PPS Mortgage Fund		3%
Strategic Finance	Moratorium	3%
Equities		
Brook		3%
Fisher Funds NZ Growth		4%

Continued

ING Equity Selection	5%
Pengana Emerging Companies	6%
Caledonia	2%
F&C US Smaller Cos	2%
JP Morgan Fleming Oseas	5%
JP Morgan Fleming European Growth	1%
Monks	4%
Platinum Int'l Fund	3%
PPS International Equities	16%
RIT Capital	3%
SVG Capital	2%
The Alliance Trust	2%

Property

ING Property Securities Fund	5%
PPS Property Fund	2%
Sovereign Col First Stat Global Property	3%

Alternatives

Liontamer Combi Series3	1%
Liontamer Brick Series1	2%
OMIP 15seven	3%
OMIP 2 Eclipse	1%
Total	100%

way, you have to wonder about the value of the certification of financial planners, and the merits of the CFP of the Year award.

The next two portfolios (pages 159–160) are also from Lyfords, although both were prepared for the same client. The combined portfolio was close to a million dollars so you might expect some sophistication from the advisor, such as seeking to hold listed shares directly rather than through unit trusts and master trusts, for example.

Here it's Lyfords' penchant to load up the portfolio with a raft of ING products — the PPS offerings are all from ING. Certainly you would be hard-pressed to find any academic portfolio work that would support such exposure to one issuer. As I'll discuss in the next chapter, however, Lyfords and ING do indeed have a 'relationship'.

7. Phillip King of Ellery Cornwell

Down the dunny went Phillip's clients with Bridgecorp. No matter — Phillip picked up his 3 per cent-plus commissions so clearly his Certified Financial Planner of the Year award in 2004 was no guarantee of competence.

When a client asked him why Australian regulators had suspended the prospectus of Bridgecorp's Australian wing, Phillip King told him that it was because they had used the wrong typeface when it was printed. King should have had access to this kind of crucial inside information, because he was a regular guest aboard *Medici*, the luxury launch that Bridgecorp subsidiary Poseidon owned and moored at Auckland's Viaduct Basin.[2]

Presumably he was reassured by the answers Bridgecorp executives gave to the searching questions he asked during these water-borne 'business meetings', because King went to extraordinary lengths to get clients into Bridgecorp Pty in Australia through Bridgecorp New Zealand, even after Bridgecorp Pty had been ordered to stop raising money from the Australian public. King presumably thought the Australian Securities and Investment Commission was pretty heavy-handed indeed if he believed what he was telling others — that it had taken the drastic action of shutting the company down simply because of using the 'Times New Roman' font. Otherwise, what was he thinking, as he stuffed clients who asked for conservative portfolios into trash like Bridgecorp and Provincial Finance? No doubt the commission will have been much on his mind.

In September 2008, Phillip sold out to IRG, but didn't manage to flick on his liabilities to disgruntled clients, which still rest with him. Let's hope IRG can rehabilitate him.

8. Ricky Bennett and Bennetts Financial Services

A portfolio constructed with loving care by Bennetts of Invercargill is shown overleaf. A massive 44 per cent of the investor's wealth sunk into this portfolio may not be recoverable, as it included the toxic waste of Bridgecorp, Provincial and Dominion (failed finance companies) and MFS Pacific (who pulled the pin on Vestar's funding,

Bennetts 2007

Description	Status	Percentage of portfolio
Cash & fixed interest		
Bennetts Fin. Services ASB Trust A/c		1%
Bridgecorp Secured Debenture	Receivership	4%
Dominion Finance	Receivership	11%
GPG Finance Capital Notes		4%
SCF Secured Debenture (8%)		10%
SCF Secured Debenture (9.15%)		20%
SFL Deb Stock		11%
Strategic Finance Ltd	Moratorium	7%
TrustPower Ltd		9%
ING Regular Income Fund	Frozen	15%
MFS Pacific Finance	Liquidation	8%
Total		100%

Bennetts 2007

Description	Status	Percentage of portfolio
Cash & Fixed Interest		
Bennetts Fin. Services ASB Trust A/c		1%
Dominion Finance	Receivership	16%
Provincial Finance	Receivership	2%
SCF Secured Debenture (8%)		11%
SFL Deb Stock		13%
Strategic Sub Notes	Moratorium	8%
ING Diversified Yield Fund	Frozen	22%
ING Regular Income Fund	Frozen	13%
Equities		
AMP Strategic Partnership		14%
Total		100%

hanging all its clientele out to dry). Much of the remainder weighs heavy with commission-laden PPS products from ING and high-commission fad funds such as Liontamer.

And if you're wondering what SFL Debenture Stock is — well, it stands for Southland Finance Limited, a company that SFL chairman and director Richard (Ricky) Bennett knows well. We're sure Ricky would have been completely upfront about telling all his punters about this related-party transaction.

If you feel sorry for the poor sod with the first of these two portfolios above, try the second one on page 162. The client here has seen 61 per cent of their hard-earned wealth go west, and why? Well, let's just note that there's not one product here that Ricky and the team don't get commissions from.

Even if we ignore the self-interest of the advisor, the portfolios betray a complete lack of any grasp of the point of diversification. There's a veritable galaxy out there when you're picking securities, outside of high-risk credit. So why go boots and all into just eight, especially when five are directly related to the local property-lending sector, and two further funds — the ING funds — are indirectly related, through their exposure to collateralised debt obligations and collateralised loan obligations.

The message: who gives a stuff about the client's well-being? Show me the money!

Bennetts are decent enough to proclaim on their website that they are a 'financial partner' with ING. 'With our new partnership with ING,' Ricky is quoted as saying, 'we can honestly say no-one can offer the depth of knowledge that Bennetts can.' And it's probably true: there are probably few Kiwi financial advisors who can boast such an encyclopaedic knowledge of what ING has to offer. But if Ricky is claiming to be anything other than a commission salesman — an independent advisor, say — then this claim must be treated with caution. After all, go to a Holden dealer, and you can be sure you'll walk away with the very best car for you — provided it's a Holden.

Of course, Ricky is a proud two-times recipient of a 'Financial Planner of the Year' award from industry trade mag, *Financial Alert*.

Bennetts displays these titles in the window of their Invercargill and Queenstown offices.

Summing it up: financial advisor swine flu

Most recessions have a cleansing effect. The great finance company collapse of the last two years has done more to expose the haemorrhagic fever afflicting New Zealand's financial advisory industry than anything else ever. And it's not a pretty sight. There's blood and pus everywhere you look.

Everyone who has ever tried their hand at investing has stuffed it up on occasions. After all, it's all about risk. If there were no risk, there would be no rewards. But there are certain rules that you should follow if you're trying to minimise your exposure to risk, and most of those rules have to do with diversification. Most of the rest have to do with working out just how great the risk you're contemplating taking really is, whether it's worth it for the potential rewards, and how much of your hard-earned cash you should chance on it. That's why research is so important.

And if you are taking these risks on someone else's behalf, then you should eat, drink and breathe these rules.

When the finance companies started falling, people got burned. Lots of the investors were DIY greedies whose eye was caught by the ads in the Sunday papers offering half a per cent per annum more than a bank call account and who clipped the coupon and mailed it off with their cheque. Some were persuaded by the slick advertising, featuring endorsements by celebrities (and if you can't trust a former All Black or newsreader, who can you trust?). Both lots deserve only limited sympathy, because they neglected to keep themselves safe from the sharks by even so much as having a quick look for cruising fins.

But others were plonked into finance companies by people who should have known better, not only because they broadcast to the public that they knew better, but also because they accepted money on the assurance to clients that they did know better. When those investments turned sour and their charred clients opened up their portfolios to scrutiny, the truth emerged. Investment choices were being skewed by, or even taken solely on the basis of, commissions offered by investment product providers.

That was one problem. But others quickly became apparent, too. The quality of the advice that people were paying for was desperately bad. The concept of diversification seemed completely alien to a good proportion of the industry. And rather than making any kind of sophisticated choices about securities — such as buying into listed stocks and bonds directly — advisors seemed to be cramming their clients' portfolios with managed funds, which came with their own set of fees and, of course, made their own decisions about what stocks and bonds to hold. So what were you paying the advisor for again?

The cases we've looked at contradict the key claims that the financial advisory industry makes — namely that advisors are independent, and that they are acting in their clients' interests. In the next chapter I'll present further reasons why these claims are false. The present meltdown offers the government a great opportunity to flush out the Augean stables and start again with a nice, clean concrete floor.

9

Independence Day

Let's continue to look at just how 'independent' the financial advice industry can claim to be. The regulator has made some effort to help investors but so far the industry is running rings around Mr Plod.

Yes commissioner, I will disclose

In the last chapter examples were used to illustrate that much of the industry that claims to be offering independent investment advice to Kiwis is compromised by the conflict of interest arising from the commissions-based income it receives. So are commissions always a bad thing? Absolutely not — I have nothing against salesmen except when they purport to be something else; in this case, financial advisors to ordinary mum-and-dad investors.

Led by the insurance multinationals who have moved their commission-based sales force into the field of financial advice, usurping the term 'financial advisor' in the process, the financial advisory industry has become fatally flawed. The travesty of justice demonstrated time and again in Chapter 7 arises because so many so-called financial advisors know next to nothing about investment markets and what makes them tick. To call themselves an 'advisor', implying to the investor off the street that they have the expertise to knowledgably advise the customer how to invest, is the core defect.

The problem's made worse, of course, by the fact that their investment 'decisions' appear time and again to be driven by where the fattest commissions are available to them. Fiduciary duty of care to the client? What's that? The conflict of interest that commissions present prevents these players from serving anyone but themselves.

For the public the lesson is clear. The façade of professionalism that these slicks have built needs to be torn asunder and the barriers to entry for the incompetent into the advisory business, raised. The regulator has started to respond, but as I'll show, has so far introduced no more than a slap with a wet bus ticket.

Financial Advisers Act 2008 and disclosure
— as through a glass, darkly

Since February 2008 all financial advisors have been obliged to make a disclosure statement available to every prospective client and to ensure that the client has read it before any 'financial advice' is proffered. The Securities Commission intended that:

> The new disclosure laws require more information to be given to clients, especially about fees and remuneration. Full disclosure must be made up-front by financial/investment advisers before investment advice is given to members of the public and by investment brokers before receiving investment money or investment property from members of the public. The disclosure is mandatory. It must be made in a disclosure statement, and provided without the client having to ask for it.

> The new rules are intended to make sure clients receive information they need about their investment advisers. In particular clients must be given more information about fees, commissions and other remuneration. This will extend to any benefits to be received by the adviser, whether from the client or another source, and include 'soft' commissions and indirect benefits relevant to the advice being given to the client.

Investment advisers' disclosure must include:

> their experience and qualifications;
> criminal convictions;
> the nature and level of fees charged;
> other interests and relationships (including all
> remuneration); and
> types of securities the adviser advises on.

Disclosure statements must be kept up-to-date and must not be deceptive, misleading or confusing.

Excellent! The required disclosure covers the lot. All it needs, to be effective, is for the customer to *read* the disclosure statement before they're permitted to receive the advice. Oh dear. The regulator has failed to standardise the disclosure requirements so investors can readily comprehend and compare them and that, as I'll demonstrate, is just bread and jam to an industry skilled in obfuscation.

Let's look at one thing that every client quite naturally wants to know, and that in any properly constructed relationship, they'd be able to find out easily and with an economy of effort. Fees! How much is it going to cost me to accept the service being offered?

The problem with disclosure statements is that all the relevant stuff like fees, expenses and remuneration is spread over various sections, including in the fine print at the very end. Ask yourself, who reads all the terms and conditions on their air ticket, or the licence agreement you scroll past when you're installing new software? And even if you're the sort of person who does, by the time you've waded through page after page of the same kind of material, it's still pretty likely you'll have exhausted your patience for legalese and be disinclined to proceed to the fine print.

Herein lies the opportunity for the white-shoe salesman — drain the reader's energy before they get the full picture. This type of stunt has been refined over the aeons by insurance companies.

Take the disclosure statement for an advisor selling AMP products — there are over 80 of them out there, and while they're promoted as 'independent', they're 'aligned' with AMP, whatever that means. The AMP agents' disclosure statement as of 23 July 2008 is 15 pages long, including the fee and commission schedules. Looking at page 2 under the section 'Relevant fees', the statement reads:

I do not currently charge my client fees direct.

Great — but what about *indirect* fees? Sure enough, the next section heading is 'Relevant Remuneration', where the statement (and what follows is taken directly from the disclosure statement and is reproduced in fine print to preserve the authenticity of the reading experience) reads:

I derive remuneration by reference to commission for the investment products I sell. The amount of commission I may derive is generally dependent on the product sold, the amount of your contributions or investment and, in some cases, the period of your contribution.

I derive renumeration by reference to all or some of the following types of commission when I sell an investment product:

- Initial commission
- Servicing commission
- Investment Product commission
- Assets Under Management commission
- Up-front commission.

The amount or rate of the renumeration I will or may derive in respect of a particular product is attached as Appendix B.

All commission is paid by the particular product provider. Commission on all products is paid from AMP through Inrich Financial Services Limited, which then pays me.

I receive a fixed semi-monthly payment of $1,110 from Inrich Financial Services Limited. Some of the funds for this payment are derived from an establishment allowance paid to Inrich Financial Services Limited by AMP. This establishment allowance consists of 24 semi-monthly payments of $1,250 and is designed to provide a base income while advisers build up their client base.

In addition to product commission or service fees, my adviser business or I may receive renumeration that consists of recognition or monetary rewards through the AMP Rewards Programme. This programme rewards AMP advisers and AMP Adviser Businesses based on sales volumes, some of which relate to sales of AMP or AMP Wrap investment products. The highest performing AMP advisers and Adviser Businesses are eligible to receive:

- a full or partial subsidy from AMP to attend an AMP offshore convention held every second year and/or an annual AMP convention held in either New Zealand or Australia;

- an individual cash prize of up to $5,000 in recognition of high sales performance in a particular product category over one year;

- an AMP Adviser Business business development payment of up to $25,000 in recognition of high performance, implementation of strategy and superior customer offering for the single champion AMP Adviser Business per year.

From time to time AMP and/or other product providers may invite me to attend functions, training and so on at no cost, or at a reduced cost, or provide me or my business with gifts. They may also run sales competitions with prizes such as cash, gift vouchers, travel vouchers and so on.

I may also receive gifts from AMP and other product providers whose products I sell, such as gift vouchers, bottles of wine, entertainment, tickets to events or participation in conferences or seminars.

The take-home message from the above, supposing you read it all, is that this agent is going to be getting a fair slice of pie, and since the only one on the table is the returns that your investment stands to make, that means it's your shout: pie all round. If, like most people, fine print makes you sleepy, you'll be ready for a bit of a lie-down by now.

But stay conscious for goodness' sake — there's more in the appendix. While this agent is not charging you fees for a sit-down chat or an annual management fee, don't be suckered into thinking that you're not really paying at all. The appendix will tell you how much of your initial investment is making their way to the agent. Still, I guess we do have the Financial Advisers Act 2008 to thank for at least informing us that AMP 'advisers' *make their money by way of commissions and receive rewards based on their sales volumes*. This is valuable information if you're trying to decide how objective the advisor is going to be in selecting products that suit you.

Wouldn't it be so much easier if the disclosure statement presented a simple number, upfront — the advisor's statutory declaration of what the maximum fees plus expenses that he or any other party from whom he received remuneration, payments of expenses or other forms of recompense would receive as a result of your investment?

Then, if they liked, they could present a second, lower number that was what they expected the *actual* number to be. So forget all the bullshit, arse-covering and escape clauses with which these institutions lace their documents — what the client needs is a very clear, one-line answer to what they must know.

How comatose is the regulator? Through the thick and opaque smog that financial institutions have led investors in recent years, it's incredible that regulatory protection for the consumer persists in being so deeply inadequate.

Let's return to the case of prominent financial advisor, and '2004 Certified Financial Planner of the Year' recipient, Alison Renfrew of Lyfords. Her comments were revealing of industry attitudes where she was quoted in the *Sunday-Star Times*.[1] Asked about sponsored trips and perks that advisors receive from the insurance companies and fund managers, Alison blurted:

> . . . such trips were not in themselves a problem. The client
> needs to know why products have been recommended
> based on research and needs to be given choices which are
> then discussed. I do not believe any of my clients would be
> disappointed to learn that because we work hard some firms
> choose to reward us via trips.

She expects us to believe the commonly peddled fiction that the booze cruises are educational trips? Alison also holds that it isn't reasonable to expect advisors to have to disclose such trips, as there were so many of them that disclosure statements to clients would have to be:

> . . . enormous and would take hours to explain to clients.

Can she be for real? Let's look at the disclosure statement for Alison and Richard Renfrew from Lyford Asset Management, which is current from 23 December 2008. It's a mere eight pages long — just the sort of light reading you need after a hard day's work, and all well worth the effort to make sure your savings aren't going to be ripped to bits.

Page 1 has all the glossy fluff, talking up qualifications, experience and the benefit of professional memberships and, of course, industry awards.

Page 2 is where it starts to get juicy, assuring you that Lyfords independently researches the products its advisors give advice on. The extensive product list that follows leaves you in no doubt that you're in reliable hands. It reveals, too, that they have an agency agreement in regards to superannuation funds and insurance bonds with Tower, Sovereign, AMP, AXA, AMP, ING, Fidelity, Asteron etc.

Hmmm. Agency arrangements. In English, that means commissions and probably sales volume bonuses, too, so that's good to know. Lucky the investing public is literate enough to be able to translate the industry lexicon. Further, it's good to know they've entered into a licence agreement with MAN Investments Pty (the promoter of OM-IP Funds) and ING (NZ) Limited, which enables them to distribute the master trust, Private Portfolio Service (which we've seen liberally sprinkled throughout the dud portfolios we were looking at in the last chapter), as well as other ING-managed or -administered funds. Each of these, of course, is a healthy source of commissions to Lyfords.

If you haven't already twigged or thrown in the towel from fatigue, here comes the boldest declaration. In a larger typeface and in bold it reads:

> LYFORDS has no obligation to place a percentage of business with any product provider. LYFORDS are independently owned and operated.

'Independent' — what a relief. Thought for a minute there, with all that talk of agencies and licence agreements they were just another bunch of commission salespeople. But no, they've promised independence and on page 3 where the real information is put forward under the heading 'Remuneration', it seems at first glance to be confirmed. The statement refers to the fact the

> Directors are on a salary and do not receive brokerage directly.

Directly? What about indirectly? Does that mean it goes into the left pocket rather than the right? If you, beleaguered investor, have the stamina to look hard enough, you'll find this admission:

> . . . any remuneration Alison or Richard receives on behalf of LYFORDS is used to pay costs incurred in providing advice eg: office, staff and marketing costs along with their personal remuneration.

It's in this kind of disingenuous clause that the Act is exposed as an ass. If you're still awake, you have to go to another section to find out what fees you'll be paying or likely to pay. In this case you need to go to Appendix D, which includes the fee schedule. Aha, you think, 'fee schedule'— OK, so I *am* going to pay fees. But then you see a blurb stating that Lyfords is eligible to receive commission, bonuses, rebates and non-monetary payments from product providers in relation to the sale of products and the use of Wrap Services. These details will be provided in yet another section, Appendices A and B. But I distinctly remember something saying they were independent and weren't we just told that they personally didn't receive brokerage? Oh no, that's right — the brokerage just goes to pay expenses that they would otherwise have had to pay personally. They have a wonderful way with words.

Gagging for more, you go straight to the other appendix where you seek a full breakdown of the fees you're likely to be paying, or the income that your now not-so-independent advisor is making from the recommended products that have been independently researched and that pay their firm commissions.

Fat chance. It's only once you've decided to become a client of firms with disclosure statements like this and the composition of your portfolio has been determined, that the advisor will paint the full picture of fees, commissions etc. that apply in your particular case. The charges are often very product-specific. There can be little doubt that mum-and-dad investors lack the information to assess what the all-up encompassing fees will be on their portfolio, and how much of their return effectively leaches to the advisor. And it's pretty unlikely Alison or Richard or anyone else at Lyfords will sit them in a chair and walk them through the entire stratigraphy of fees, commissions, perks, trips, sweeteners, rebates, bonuses, prizes etc. etc. that they're rubbing their hands over. All that stuff is in the disclosure statement, right? Their conscience is clear and — this is only a slightly higher standard — their legal obligations are discharged as soon as you sign to say you've read it.

The Act obliges 'advisers' to disclose their vested interests, but doesn't obligate them to disclose them in a manner where the information is actually conveyed. Before you let a perfect stranger tie a rubber band to your ankle and push you off a bridge, you tend to sign a waiver. Your life is at stake when you do a bungy jump, but the entire document is only an A4 page in plain English. By contrast, the kind of smart-arse documentation evolved in the moral compost heap that is the insurance industry and readily adapted to the financial advisory industry is designed to tie the public in knots well before they get to the truth.

The Australian experience suggests that nothing short of a radical change in the entire regulatory framework will purge the savings and investment industry of the abuse of commissions. In that same *Sunday Star-Times* article, it was reported:

> David Whitely from the Industry Funds Association in Australia, which provides top-performing super funds that are run on a not-for-profit basis and do not pay commission to advisers, says tougher disclosure rules introduced in Australia at that time had done nothing to stamp out conflicts of interest.
>
> According to super funds ratings agencies, the most recent data shows nine of the top 10 best performing funds over one and five years are industry funds. 'But not one of the top 30 financial planning companies recommends them because they don't pay commission,' he said. 'There's a huge conflict of interest. Advisers have to choose whether they give advice that's in the best interests of their clients or which pays them commission, and they choose commission every time.'
>
> A study by the Australian Securities & Investments Commission found that in 4900 super fund switching recommendations given by advisers, 90% recommended a switch to a related fund on which they earned commission. In many cases they made only generalised references to costs and failed to report on lost benefits.
>
> Whitely said the only way to turn what was in effect a sales channel for product producers into an independent professional advice channel was to change the law to require financial intermediaries to act in the best interests of their client.
>
> Overnight, commission as a form of remuneration would disappear, he said, though he admitted the Australian government was not a supporter of such a move.

The paper reported that the insurers and advisors talked to in New Zealand said that any move to introduce an equivalent measure here 'would decimate' the advisory industry, 'as people simply did not want to write out cheques for advice'. Therein lies the rub — people won't pay for something they perceive has no value-add, and that reduces this type of pretend advisor to getting their pay from commissions and kick-backs from product issuers. In other words, there is no case whatsoever that they are providing anything an investor would actually pay for — they acknowledge it. Where are you Mr/Ms Regulator? These disclosure documents are not doing the job.

Independent and authoritative investment ratings — yeah right!

Even the most rugged of individuals in the financial industry might find their determination to be an 'independent' advisor crumple in the face of some of the commissions on offer. After all, if you don't have much of a clue about what makes one product better than another, or of how to set about finding out, why not plug your clients into the fund whose provider is promising to spirit you away on the kind of luxury getaway a hardworking expert like you deserves?

We've already covered in Chapter 6 the worthlessness of the bouquets dished out by the various industry suppliers such as rating agencies and industry magazines. But what of another feature that fund industry suppliers sell, namely their fund ratings? Are they any use to the investing public?

Most people are familiar with 'the Big Three' international credit ratings agencies of Standard & Poor's, Moody's and Fitch. You occasionally see their ratings affixed to New Zealand companies — Hanover Finance, for example, wore their BB rating from Fitch with pride (even though it spells 'junk bond' if you look up Fitch's scale to see what they mean by it). They wore it with pride right up until they announced that they couldn't pay everyone their money, let alone the interest on their money, after all.

We have our own, local versions. Morningstar, for example, undertakes research into investment products and provides opinions and ratings to subscribers. FundSource, currently owned by the New Zealand Stock Exchange, does the same.

But there's a growing disillusionment with ratings agencies in general — the Big Three have emerged from the present global meltdown with more than a little egg on their faces after continuing to assign AAA ratings to a good proportion of the firms that crashed and burned and took the world economy with them. Locally, Morningstar is cynically referred to in the industry as 'Morning-after-star', a reflection of the dawning realisation that it (like the Big Three American agencies, and like FundSource) is a lagging rather than a leading indicator. They can, that is, tell you what has happened in the past, but their ratings are somewhat less reliable for the purposes of investing for the future.

Nonetheless, it is becoming very clear that inadequately resourced financial advisors have been over-relying on rating agency research. Let's have a look at a couple of examples of where a financial advisor has slavishly followed ratings agency recommendations, to their cost — or, let's be accurate, to their client's detriment.

1. Wealthy and Wise

One of the more eye-catching aspects of the portfolio on the next page is the number of ING products it contains. On their website the firm tells us that they rely on ratings from Morningstar Research Group and Mercers. Also they use Strategi and the Portfolio Group of ING (NZ). Strategi's 'sole permitted financial services client' is ING (NZ) Ltd.

Some 34 per cent of this portfolio is either frozen or in receivership — ING Diversified Yield Fund and Capital + Merchant. Capital + Merchant were paying around 3 per cent commission to the advisor, OM-IP pay 4–5 per cent and PPS also pay handsome commissions. Almost half of the portfolio is with one issuer, ING.

So, like the portfolios covered in the previous chapter this one has ended up concentrated heavily in commission-laced products. But what the advisor is telling us is that they are not making those

Wealthy and Wise 2007

Description	Status	Percentage of portfolio
Cash & fixed interest		
Macquarie GEAA (access account)		8%
Capital Merchant Sec Deb	Receivership	16%
ING Diversified Yield Fund	Frozen	18%
Property		
PPS Property Fund		7%
Equities		
WBC Banking Corp		9%
PPS Australia Equities		11%
PPS NZ Equities		2%
PPS Platinum International		5%
PPS International Equities		5%
Alternative		
OMIP 150 Fund		3%
OMIP series5		16%
Total		100%

calls. Rather they are the result of advice and recommendations they subscribe to from the ratings agencies, Strategi, and the Portfolio Group of ING (NZ) Ltd.

Can there be some sort of tie-up between the supposedly 'independent' research house Morningstar — relied upon by a horde of 'independent' advisors who need to be told what to think about investment products — and ING?

Following the freezing of ING's Diversified Yield Fund (DYF) and Regular Income Fund (RIF), the trade magazine *Financial Alert* set out to explore the portfolios that Morningstar had drawn up at the request of ING for the use of its network of 'affiliated' advisors — such as Wealthy and Wise. These continued to feature ING's DYF and RIF right up until they went belly-up, not a great endorsement of the 'research' prowess of Morningstar at all.

According to *Financial Alert,* 19 March 2009:

> In documents obtained by Financial Alert, Morningstar's June 2007 income-biased model portfolios prepared for ING-affiliated financial advisers featured a 25% allocation to the RIF for defensive, conservative, and balanced portfolio and a 19% and 10% allocation for growth and aggressive portfolios respectively. In 2006, the model portfolios had a 20% allocation to the ING DYF for defensive and conservative portfolios, reducing to 10% for balanced and growth investors, and 4% for aggressive income-biased investors.

Some 18 per cent of the above balanced portfolio is in DYF. Each year Morningstar publishes a strategy handbook that is sold to advisory firms across New Zealand. The April 2007 edition of Morningstar's strategy handbook didn't include — let alone rate — ING's DYF or RIF in the overall generic research. Yet it was happy to recommend these fixed-interest products to ING's 'affiliated advisors'. What gives?

The answer is that Morningstar Consulting is available for hire by fund managers and advisors to advise on portfolio construction. In this capacity it worked with ING's 'affiliated' advisor groups to work up portfolio recommendations full of ING product. It says that it provided:

> . . . advice on certain product selection issues

though this is influenced too by

> adviser feedback.[2]

So presumably because ING asked them to fill up the portfolio recommendations for ING-affiliated advisors with ING product, they did. What some people will do for a few pieces of silver. Apart from demonstrating how readily compromised a rating agency can be, doesn't this just bring into question once again the whole issue of who advisors really work for — clearly not just their clients.

And the Wealthy and Wise approach isn't unique. We have the portfolio of another 'independent advisor' with an ING agency arrangement that put 35 per cent of his client's portfolio into the DYF and had 60 per cent of that portfolio in ING. The issue here is that we have what are in essence commission-based salespeople promoting themselves to the public as investment advisors. It would be difficult to find any academic text on portfolio theory that recommended that such exposure to a single issuer was in any way prudent.

2. Financial Edge Planning

Deferring to the so-called expertise of rating agencies is endemic in the financial advisory business. An extract from a 'financial plan' prepared by Financial Edge Planning, which we were given to run the ruler over before the investor plunged their hard-earned savings into it, is shown on pages 182–83. Note that all recommendations are justified by recommendations from research houses.

But it's the same old stuff that we've seen earlier in this chapter and in Chapter 8. The date of recommendation was 3 March 2008, so just before all hell broke loose internationally, but well into the New Zealand finance company debacle, when alarm bells could be said to have been ringing.

Points to note:

▷ The ING Regular Income Fund was frozen on 12 March 2008 — nine days after the plan was prepared! ING Enhanced Yield Fund and ING Credit Opportunities Fund — recommended and rated by Morningstar — have also since been frozen.

▷ Some 51 per cent of the portfolio is allocated toward ING Funds, which makes it closely resemble the 'model portfolios' prepared for ING by Morningstar and turned up by *Financial Alert*'s investigation.

▷ Within the prepared financial plan, a 'summary of investments' was provided that promoted the funds' 'good liquidity'. So sad. If the investor had relied on this advisor's advice, they would have had 12 per cent of their funds written off or 'frozen' before they even saw the end of 2008.

Financial Edge Planning state on their website:

> Our philosophy is to grow our clients' wealth by using a holistic approach to financial planning. We realize that each person has a different outlook on financial matters which requires individual attention. As a boutique financial planning company we understand our clients' individual needs and tailor advice to suit.
>
> To do this we take time to understand our clients' individual financial situation, their objectives, goals and needs. We then develop a comprehensive plan addressing each area of their financial world and provide prudent recommendations based on research and experience.
>
> Our investment philosophy adheres to the principle of Modern Portfolio Theory, that is, to create a portfolio structured around diversification of and within asset classes. In essence we try to maximize return for any given level of risk.

It says all the right things. They've got a philosophy. They take a holistic approach, and baby boomers like holism. 'Prudent recommendations based on research and experience.' We like that, too, and the references to 'Modern Portfolio Theory'. But all the buzzwords and warm fuzzies simply don't square with the quality of the portfolio this client nearly ended up with. Even as Financial Edge were doing the firm handshake and crinkly smile thing, funds were freezing over!

It's about accountability

What do the results of the last two chapters tell investors? The financial advisory sector is a disaster!

Remember the Imperial portfolio that had 28 per cent of the

Financial Edge Planning

Company	Fund	Weighting percentage
NBNZ	cash	3%
NBNZ	Thoroughbred Cash	10%
ING	Enhanced Yield	8%
AMP Capital	Enhanced Yield	5%
ING	PPS Mortgage Fund	5%
Rabobank	Perpetual Bond	5%
ING	Regular Income	3%
ING	Credit opportunities	1%
ING	PPS International fixed interest	3%
LM	Currency Protected Income	3%
ING	PPS Property	3%
AMP	Office Trust	1%
ING	PPS Trans Tasman Equities	4%
ING	PPS Australian Equities	9%
Brook	Alpha	4%
ING	PPS International Equities	12%
ING	PPS Asian Equities	3%
Platinum	International	7%
HunterHall	Value Growth	6%
OM-IP	3Eclipse Limited	5%
Total		100%

Asset class	Comment
Cash	OneAnswer wrap account cash hub
Cash	PIE cash fund
NZ fixed interest	Recommended rating by Morningstar
NZ fixed interest	
NZ fixed interest	Recommended by Mercers
NZ fixed interest	S&P AA rating
NZ fixed interest	Investments S&P BBB rated
International fixed interest	Rated investment grade by Morningstar
International fixed interest	Recommended by Mercers
International fixed interest	4 star rating Morningstar
International Property	Recommended by Mercers
Listed Property	FNZ rate BUY
Australasian equities	Recommended by Mercers
Australasian equities	Recommended by Mercers
Australasian equities	Recommended rating by Morningstar
International equities	Recommended by Mercers
International equities	Recommended by Mercers
International equities	4 star rating Morningstar
International equities	5 star rating Morningstar
International equities/specialty	Recommended rating by Lonsec

portfolio allocated to the RIF? And the Wealthy and Wise portfolio on page 178 with 16 per cent allocation to DYF? These are very large allocations to make to one fund and just on those grounds alone the expertise of the advisors is questionable.

And remember Bennetts of Invercargill? It's so easy to see why so much wealth has gone down the toilet in Southland: one portfolio featured 15 per cent allocated to RIF and another portfolio allocated 22 per cent to the DYF and 13 per cent to the RIF — effectively 35 per cent to funds recommended by Morningstar only to become fallen stars — frozen!

It matters not apparently whether advisors go it alone or are affiliated to a big foreign conglomerate like ING, the clients are ending up with portfolios heavily laden with commission-paying funds and with far too much concentration in too few managers. The interests of the product providers are in no way aligned to those of the saver/investor client, but it's cruel to watch just how compromised the advisory firms allow themselves to be. The question has to be asked about their fitness to practise.

While we have picked out quite a few operators in the investment advisory and financial planning industry above to illustrate what's wrong, it wouldn't be fair to suggest that these case studies are in any way exhaustive. There's a swarm of advisors out there delivering parlous value-add to clients. A gallery of the sector's leading lights demonstrates the point:

▷ Roger Moses and Graham Stevens are past presidents and current life members of the Institute of Financial Advisers. They went on to become directors of Reeves Moses Contributory Mortgages (which lost around $20 million of capital) and were directors of Nathan Finance (in receivership).

▷ Muriel Dunn (Muriel Dunn Financial Services) and Kelvin Syms (Vestar) were two of the highest-profile IFA members of their time. Both sold Bridgecorp, CMF, MFS (which was a related party) and (in Dunn's case) Five Star, often leaving clients with virtually no other investments.

▷ Ricky Bennett, Philip Holland, Phillip King and Alison Renfrew have all won awards from the IFA and been put on a pedestal. Bennett sold Bridgecorp and ING's frozen funds; Holland sold Bridgecorp, Canterbury Mortgage Fund and MFS (double brokerage), and charged a fee on top; King, the same; Renfrew sold Bridgecorp and frozen ING.

Markets can only function efficiently if the information available to both sides of a transaction is of equal quality. The investment and savings industry is racked with conflicts. The rating agencies are symptomatic of the disease — paid by issuers rather than investors, they pretend to have authority and independence. And the industry promotes their endorsements to the public in that vein. The public is the victim.

In the US the SEC has this type of behaviour under serious investigation. But it is just one of a number of misrepresentations that the savings and investment industry makes. It has to stop.

10

Regulatory
sleepwalkers

It's one of the legacies of the particular nanny-state brand of socialism that New Zealand has had for the best part of 100 years that we tend to look to the government to fix everything we perceive to be wrong with our lives. In the financial world, you see it in the wake of every finance company collapse: the tearful insistence that this shouldn't have been allowed to happen, and that the government should make it all better again.

While this argument is almost without merit — it's your money, and the onus is on you to do everything in your power to ensure you know exactly what you're doing with it when you invest — it's not completely bereft of worth. Because policy negligence has contributed in large part to the dire financial straits that not just the hapless investors in Bridgecorp, Hanover and the ANZ/ING Diversified Yield Fund find themselves in, but also the wider economy, there is more than a little culpability to be laid at the door of the policy wonks.

And it's not just the New Zealand regulator who must shoulder some of the blame for the mess we're all in at the moment. Regulators throughout the developed world ought right now to be taking the look-yourself-in-the-mirror test and asking why they didn't do things very differently in the recent past. With luck, they're even now resolving to do things very differently in the future.

Central banks

Central banks have overseen the steady deterioration of credit markets and the excesses throughout the world's financial system that have come about as the direct result of over-available credit. This has only been possible by sacrificing traditional collateral-based lending, which by 2008 had long faded as the core business of retail banks. Instead, banking has been dominated of late by transaction-driven fee generation, fee generation through counter-party participation in derivatives contracts (and if you don't know what that means, don't worry: half the people involved in doing it don't, either), and lending based solely upon a customer's perceived ability to pay — all made possible by the over-easy availability of credit. Central banks have facilitated the change.

The negligence that sponsored the ever-worsening addiction to credit across many economies began soon after the financial deregulation of the early 1980s and led inexorably to the virtual collapse of the international financial system in 2008. Ironically, one indicator of two decades of poor-quality central banking has been the spectacle of central bank governors issuing repeated public admonishments of market excesses, especially in the residential property market. Yet those excesses were a completely predictable result of slack central banking, and these same central bank leaders failed to do anything other than bleat about it.

And in doing nothing about it — indeed, in exacerbating it — it's the central banks that drove the situation finally to collapse. Their standard reaction to the merest whiff of a slowdown was to inject further liquidity into their respective economies. The governing creed had become growth — growth now and forever, world without end, amen. This inevitably created what economists call a 'moral hazard': the classic example being the situation where someone who knows their car is fully insured, say, drives more recklessly than they might if they knew they were fully exposed to the risk of damaging it. By stepping in to fix any looming slowdown every time one threatened, central banks were basically saying to those sectors of the market that were indulging in undue risks that there was no downside. 'Growth at all times at whatever cost' deserves to be the epitaph for the central bank leaders of this era; collectively and individually, their management has been incompetent — a disgrace.

Alan Greenspan, the former chairman of the US Federal Reserve, has recently admitted that he had thought the explosion of debt products would not lead to a marked deterioration in the quality of credit, because the risk would be spread across the whole economy via securitisation. He has described this assumption as one of the costliest mistakes of the whole debacle. Instead these 'assets' ended up staying largely in the hands of the financial sector. The implosion of banks and near-banks, shadow banks, and swindlers is there for all to see.

In February 2009, Mervyn King, governor of the Bank of England, delivered a similar mea culpa when he acknowledged after an enquiry from British MPs that every regulator:

> had failed to spot the seriousness of the risk-taking that was going on.

He went further, saying:

> The lesson I would draw from this is not to expect too much from regulators

and that if a watchdog had spoken up about the risk-taking:

> they would have been seen to be arguing against success.

A 2009 review by Lord Turner, the chairman of the UK's Financial Services Authority (FSA), described the present meltdown as 'arguably the worst crisis since the development of modern capitalism', and decided that what had gone so badly wrong was that the huge imbalances between nations of savers and borrowers (remember the graph on page 36 in Chapter 2) had been met head-on:

> . . . by financial innovation, with the explosion of the alphabet soup of structured credit and credit derivatives — predicated on the belief that by slicing and structuring and hedging, we could deliver to end investors combinations of risk and return

more attractive than the underlying credits.

Instead, the result has been that there has been:

hugely increased systemic risk.

Turner chastised the watchdogs for their failure to challenge the banks on their delirious optimism. What an indictment of mass central banking failure!

The review concluded that:

In the UK it's not unfair to say that:

- The Bank of England tended to focus on monetary policy defined as using the interest rate lever to hit the inflation target.

- The FSA concentrated too much on the supervision of individual institutions, not sectoral- or economy-wide trends.

- And the analysis of macro-prudential risks fell into the gap.

In New Zealand, the analysis of prudential risks didn't fall into the gap, because there was no such analysis.

The Reserve Bank of New Zealand

Here in New Zealand, the prudential supervision of the commercial banks has been just as bad. It's precipitated a marked deterioration in what used to be the collateralised lending that the banks offer (that is, the extension of loans only to those who have the assets to take as security, rather than the exclusive focus on the borrower's ability to service the loan). Central bank-supervised commercial banks have typically reduced the collateral backing requirement of their mortgages, for example, from a 30 per cent deposit to 10 per cent or even less. Accordingly, mortgage finance boomed and on the back of that, we saw enormous upward pressure on house prices. Reserve Bank prudential supervision of the institutions, whose depositors invest on the implicit (and now explicit) understanding of a central bank guarantee, has in essence been absent by historical standards. But if you were waiting for any kind of admission of fault from our last two Reserve Bank governors, equivalent to those the UK and US governors have had the courage to make, you'd be waiting still.

As happened elsewhere, both governors Don Brash and Alan Bollard deplored the frenzy in the residential property market — the most high-profile demonstration of the credit-funded speculative excess of their times — yet both dumbly claimed that asset bubbles were not the preserve of Reserve Bank policy. Neither seems to have paused for a moment to consider that the deterioration of prudential supervision that occurred on their watch has been the cause. It's ironic that this should have happened in a jurisdiction that skited to the world about how accountable its central bank leadership was for performance.

In short, both governors are fully culpable — whether through incompetence or plain ignorance. That they're too timid to acknowledge that the bubble originated with their management (or lack thereof) is no reason for the public to overlook the source of the problem. Let's hope future governors are more conscious that they draw half-million- dollar salaries for more than getting out of bed each morning.

What needs to happen with central banking? The most important line to be redrawn is between those banks that are under direct prudential supervision of the central bank, and in which the depositing public can justifiably have confidence that their deposits are 'safe', and all other financial institutions where the safety of deposits isn't guaranteed but dependent on the risk profile of their lending and investment books.

That, of course, is not what's happened. The Reserve Bank has extended an explicit government guarantee beyond the banking sector — a move necessitated by the panicked state of markets at that time. However, once the emergency has passed, it has a responsibility to effectively pull that liability — which falls ultimately on taxpayers

— back to the banking sector. Further, the RBNZ needs to overhaul the prudential requirements on all banks and rein them back to the standards that those institutions were required to meet before this period of mass central-bank incompetence broke out. Banks should be in the business of collateralised lending only, so that the explicit guarantee to depositors — a charge on taxpayers — need never be called on. The chances of depositors at banks being out-of-pocket should be negligible — not because the poor old taxpayer will always be there to take the hit, but because the Reserve Bank is doing its supervisory job properly.

Out of adversity comes opportunity

If we can agree that the financial sector rules and supervision have been exposed as utterly inadequate and in need not just of an overhaul, but also of a rewrite, then it's not difficult to see that there's an enormous opportunity here for New Zealand to set the new gold standard for financial market behaviour. This could be the opportunity to establish us as a centre of regulatory excellence, a Swiss-style haven of safety for investors. After all, most other financial systems are on their knees as well, so the time is right. Our finance company sector is clearly our version of the subprime debacle — that this cancer hasn't brought down our banking system as well is due solely to the fact that house prices in New Zealand have yet to revert to sustainable levels. But hold onto your hats: the ongoing global deleveraging will expose our bank balance sheets as fragile.

If you mean to rebuild a robust and functional financial system, you'll need not only to restore competent central banking practices but also set in place the ethical foundations upon which such a system is based. That standard of behaviour — which has to be instilled in all participants — has to be at the forefront of the system's design, and in the end will determine whether it's a global centre of excellence or not. We've got a long way to go. Speaking about the finance company sector, the New Zealand Registrar of Companies has outlined an environment where these companies were:

> masking the true performance of their loan portfolio
>
> engaged in excessive related-party lending

and that in some cases

> the only objective of entering into one of these transactions
> was to benefit one of the directors (or interests associated with
> the director) or prop up a poor[ly] performing investment.

Bad enough that some of the directors of these companies were happy to indulge in this sort of behaviour. Far worse that through laziness or incompetence, it seems that independent directors of these companies allowed it to go on, too. I think that the fiduciary duty of care that these directors owe to those from whom they're raising money was trampled roughshod.

It's not enough for the government to promise to crack down on these cases in future: there's plenty of scope under current law to bring charges against those involved, including some who I consider to be lazy directors who show up for board meetings because it looks good on their CV. But the opportunity, of course, is to instil the opposite set of ethics across the finance sector and to aspire to make it a centre of excellence rather than a den of iniquity. Undoubtedly, this will involve a change of personnel, as it's difficult, just like that, to get a leopard to change its spots.

Ethics and financial markets — from rules-based to principles-based regulation

At the centre of the outbreak of financial market skulduggery in New Zealand has been a propensity for directors to condone behaviour that is legal but morally wrong. Encouraged by the elasticity and the porosity of the rules governing the sector — to say nothing, because we've already said so much, of the negligence of the regulator — a mass breakdown of ethical standards seems to have developed, which is why so many depositors with these companies have been done over like a dog's dinner.

Some of the largest finance companies were taking in money,

lending it to companies associated with directors on non-commercial terms (such as where all interest was capitalised, so that the borrower only paid interest when they paid back the loan — often many years into the future). Then the company would run a heavy public advertising campaign, in most cases given momentum by a celebrity endorsement — while all the time the interest to debenture and deposit holders was simply paid from new money coming in the door.

This kind of 'Ponzi scheme' is not really business at all. It's a swindle, no different from anything Bernie Madoff was getting up to in the US. All the same, it's legal, and that's really where you rely on the integrity of someone in the boardroom to object. It won't be any director — the swindlers themselves would be the last the public could rely on — so it should be an independent director. But even then there's no guarantee, certainly not if these independents have been drawn from the usual line-up of rent-a-director boardroom journeymen.

To hammer this accountability home and give mum-and-dad investors some protection, we need to reverse the incentives. Rather than establish a labyrinth of laws and regulations that try to anticipate everything a bank or non-bank finance-sector company and its directors can or can't do when they take in money from the public, what's needed is a sharp reminder of what is ethical and what is not. Such a 'sharp' reminder would be there if unethical behaviour landed directors with unlimited personal liability.

This is at the core of what's known as 'principles-based regulation', and in the UK, for example, it has lately been preferred to the 'rules-based regulation' that is paramount in New Zealand and Australia. The big problem with rules-based regulation is that regulators set the rules, only for sharp operators in the private sector to throw themselves into the challenge of trying to work out how to bend, evade or manipulate those rules for profit. This relies on the regulator keeping ahead of the private sector's combined capacity to fox the rules. In a tiny jurisdiction like New Zealand, the regulator is so unlikely to be equal to that particular task that it's a wonder we've persisted with a rules-based approach for so long.

So what are the principles that regulators should enshrine as fundamental, such that they can then threaten any financial market offender with dire consequences should they breach them?

Here they are, directly from Britain's FSA (Financial Services Authority):[1]

The Principles

1 **Integrity**

A firm must conduct its business with integrity.

2 **Skill, care and diligence**

A firm must conduct its business with due skill, care and diligence.

3 **Management and control**

A firm must take reasonable care to organise and control its affairs responsibly and effectively, with adequate risk management systems.

4 **Financial prudence**

A firm must maintain adequate financial resources.

5 **Market conduct**

A firm must observe proper standards of market conduct.

6 **Customers' interests**

A firm must pay due regard to the interests of its customers and treat them fairly.

7 **Communications with clients**

A firm must pay due regard to the information needs of its clients, and communicate information to them in a way which is clear, fair and not misleading.

8 **Conflicts of interest**

A firm must manage conflicts of interest fairly, both between itself and its customers and between a customer and another client.

9 **Customers: relationships of trust**

A firm must take reasonable care to ensure the suitability of its advice and discretionary decisions for any customer who is entitled to rely upon its judgment.

10 **Clients' assets**

A firm must arrange adequate protection for clients' assets when it is responsible for them.

11   Relations with regulators

A firm must deal with its regulators in an open and cooperative way, and must disclose to the FSA appropriately anything relating to the firm of which the FSA would reasonably expect notice.

Notice principle number 6 — it's the fiduciary duty of care requirement, that is so openly flaunted in New Zealand by banks, finance companies and fund managers.

We've seen an example of reversing the incentives in New Zealand's relatively recent past. Like Mussolini, who made Italian trains run on time, Roger Douglas got a few things right in his time in the Minister of Finance role. Early in his stint, he came up against the situation where tax regulators had been running around busily trying to come up with rules to stop sophisticated investors arbitraging our tax regime by investing abroad — using partnerships, blind trusts, tax haven entities of every description — to avoid the impost of tax here in New Zealand. Douglas dealt to it in a single move, by reversing the incentives. He inserted a simple statutory declaration in your annual tax return that obliged you to declare that you or your related parties had no financial interests whatsoever in overseas entities other than those already declared in the return.

In other words, the onus of proof was suddenly on the taxpayer to swear that they hadn't omitted to declare any income from offshore interests that might be taxable in New Zealand. The consequences of making a false declaration were severe, and far less arguable than some of the convoluted tax evasion structures that were carefully crafted to stop wrongdoing.

A principles-based approach to the regulation of New Zealand finance-sector firms and their directors, then, would have the directors sign off the 11 principles above each year, with no ability to limit their liability should they be found in breach. That should be sufficient to ensure a significant lift out of the gutter of malfeasance into which this sector has slumped.

This is what occurred some time ago in the UK — the focus of enforcement there has shifted from taking enforcement action against rule breaches, supported by breaches of principles, to enforcement against the breaches of the high-level principles, as evidenced by rule breaches; quite the opposite emphasis.

The structure of funds

Another, less fundamental but no less urgent reform that is needed is to address some of the sharp practices rife in the savings and investment sector. As shown in previous chapters, this industry is dominated by foreign insurance and banking conglomerates, which have imported many of the practices developed by the global insurance sector, even though they are inappropriate in the context of the care of savings. The single largest distortion is the loss of property rights for investors.

It is the convention that savers contributing their monies to investment funds immediately lose ownership of their property. They are exchanging their money for a claim or an entitlement to units in the fund they invest in. The safeguards that ensure the integrity of care of those savings are woefully inadequate, with the consequence that there's widespread abuse on the part of the guardians of the funds. We cannot say it is an abuse of property rights because the saver/investor is cleverly induced to forsake those when they transact with these intermediaries. Ultimately, though, because of the way their expropriated property was dealt with while under the 'care' of these funds, it *is* an abuse of property rights.

The problem is that the entity that receives the investor monies has a legal life of its own, and the trustees that are appointed to it — let alone the manager of the fund — are solely focused on the welfare of the fund as a whole, not on the rights in equity and fairness of each and every separate unitholder. This is the first abuse. It's not always the case that what's good for the fund, or its future unitholders, is good for current or past unitholders, so it becomes a matter of discretion for the manager and trustees to decide whose welfare they will promote and whose they will disregard. This is the tragedy of these discretionary trusts — such as superannuation schemes and unit trusts. It's not uncommon for trustees to make decisions that are palpably contrary to the interests of some members (or unitholders), even if they serve the interests of others.

Furthermore, the unitised structure is opaque to the investor trying to gauge what is happening to their money. There's no way, just by reviewing the movements in the price of units, that they can validate the transactions that the fund has made and the pricing of those transactions. It's common for there to be no system whereby the pricing of units is audited.

It's no coincidence, given the inordinate power that the manager has, and the absence of any binding obligation upon the trustee to protect the rights of individual unitholders, aggravated by the total opacity that the practice of unitisation affords, that these entities so badly underperform in investment markets. High and undisclosed fees and expenses are part of it, as is the manipulation of reserves that ultimately serve to further the financial position of the manager. These are all practices that the insurance industry has 'gifted' to the savings industry.

The issue is how do regulators address what is in fact, if not in law, this misappropriation of other people's property? The key is to break the role of the intermediary that sits between a saver/investor and their money. These structures are discretionary trusts — the manager and the trustees have discretion and they need to be far more transparent to members so that the abuse of the property rights of an individual member or unitholder cannot go unnoticed. It's clear that trustees are dysfunctional in this regard. If sufficient transparency to enable the sovereign rights of investor/savers is to be restored in this sector, three things are required:

▷ Instead of permitting a discretionary trust to sit between a saver/ investor and their money, the use of a bare (or non-discretionary) trust to aggregate investors' monies would be infinitely preferable. This removes the legal ability of managers and trustees to abuse the rights and entitlements of individual members in the name of 'the greater interest of the trust', as they do now.

▷ Unitisation as a practice needs to be outlawed. There's no reason whatsoever for it. Fund managers use the limp excuse of practicality, but this argument has no merit. A saver/investor should be able to see on a continuous basis how much of every security in the portfolio of the bare nominee is beneficially theirs. Further, they should be able to see every transaction — what volume, and at what price — of every security trade that takes place.

With 100 per cent transparency over their monies, there's no way the investment manager can possibly skim monies from one person's portfolio into reserves or fees or expenses, or into another portfolio, without it being detectable. Substantial benefits would arise from these changes.

Investor confidence will rise if they're able to validate independently every transaction on their portfolio. Investor financial literacy — a prerequisite for a sound, functioning savings and investment sector — will be raised exponentially if investors can have total and complete transparency over their property. Letting people see what's going on is likely to be far more effective in raising standards of financial literacy than the pink-nosed mouse that features in the advertising blitz conducted by the Office of the Retirement Commissioner.

Furthermore, and of equal importance, this transparency will compel fund managers to restrict their activities to what they're paid for — tending and caring for the financial gardens of their members, not running away with the pot plants. Trustees in this model become redundant — rather than required yet utterly ineffectual. The combination of principles-based regulation, under which individuals engaged in the provision of financial services simply go to jail if they breach their annual undertaking to maintain fiduciary care, and total transparency for investors really is nothing more than a first-principles approach to promoting ethical stanrdards in the financial sector — standards that have for far too long been trampled into the mud by those anxious to get their noses into the trough.

▷ Finally, there's the issue of product fees. The regulators have tried to address the inscrutability of true product costs by beefing up disclosure documentation. But just as we see with any rules-based regulation, this has resulted in product providers (and financial advisors, for that matter) simply producing obfuscatory disclosure statements that are little better than non-disclosure, for all the use they are in conveying information. As we saw in Chapter 9, disclosure documents commonly scatter the different components of charges throughout several sections of a long, complicated document, obliging the reader to muster them all together and try to compile them into a coherent list, from which they can begin to deduce what the true charges are. Again, and as we saw in that chapter, it's seldom possible to get close to a meaningful number until the product's details have been finalised.

The way to solve this deliberate obfuscation by the industry is to compel them to declare in a single, prominent number what the maximum charge can be. Thereafter, they can offer their raft of excuses as to why it could turn out lower. In other words, put the onus of proof on the party that has the inordinate market power in this regard. Of course, what you will see is that product-charging mechanisms change so that providers can compete under a regime that is far fairer to the consumer.

Now expect banks and insurance companies to scream loud and long about all this stuff. That'll be the first sign we're making progress. What's happening here is that regulators are simply producing constraints on the abuse of market power, which multinational companies commit to further their wealth at the expense of others. Measures of the quantity of funds being diverted into the savings and investment industry have little meaning for our national wealth when the industry charged with looking after those funds is so focused on expropriating them. Such wealth transfers do not contribute to economic growth; they're the result of a dysfunctional market.

Investment advisors and financial planners

The core shortcoming of this sector is the distance between what it is and what it says it is. It's as perfect a misrepresentation as the financial sector has managed to concoct, which is really saying something, given how grossly the industry has misled the investing public in recent years.

A large proportion of those calling themselves investment advisors and financial planners are not advisors at all. They're commissioned salespeople for investment funds. Yet they're allowed to promote themselves to the public as advisors, while their portfolio recommendations are driven by whichever providers are offering the fattest commissions. This duplicity is something the regulators should have dealt to aeons ago, but as with so much that should be regulated in the financial sector, the regulators seem in awe of the financial institutions and pay far too little attention to consumers' rights. The consequences are all around us.

Why have the regulators been so slack? One can only assume that lack of resourcing and training has led regulators to rely heavily on the resources of the industry itself when investigating and assessing industry practices. That, of course, has got them nowhere.

The word 'advisor' should be severely restricted in its application in the financial services industry. It needs to be a valued title available to be used only by those practitioners that receive 100 per cent of their remuneration from fees paid directly by those whom they advise. In other words, they should charge exactly as doctors, lawyers and accountants charge: a direct exchange of money for the service rendered. You really have to wonder what is so hard about this.

There's less actual dishonesty in this sector than the number of ministerial witch-hunts and protests from the regulator would have you believe. The primary problem is one of competence, or rather, the widespread lack of it. Most advisors have no knowledge whatsoever of economics or investment markets. They're product salesmen, trained by the industry to flog product. That they're allowed to hold themselves forth as anything other than that — and certainly as people whose expertise investors can trust — is a failure on the part of the regulator. Simply controlling the use of the term 'advisor' will go a long way to purging this sector of the charlatans and insurance salesmen who dominate it.

The supervisory bodies

We don't lack these, but collectively, they have clearly failed in recent times to protect the investing public. The question thus becomes whether the bodies themselves are impotent or whether the laws and regulations render them helpless in curbing the excesses prevalent in financial markets. Are they, in other words, just ambulances at the bottom of the cliff, trying to fix things up after the event?

Let's look at the offices of the relevant ombudsmen. They are paid for by the industry and are answerable to a board that comprises industry and consumer representatives, but are presided over by an independent chair, such as a retired judge. The ombudsmen deal with individual complaints and have powers to make binding settlements. So if a customer of the sector has a complaint, then rather than their only recourse being to the courts —which are invariably beyond the resources of an individual complainant to afford, especially when the opponent is a massively-resourced financial institution — the ombudsman represents an opportunity for the aggrieved to air their complaint before an independent authority. The ombudsman does have the power to provide redress and the financial institution upon which a judgment is delivered is bound to comply.

The biggest weakness in the ombudsman system is its confidentiality provisions. Ombudsmen have the discretion to publish findings if they are deemed in the public interest, but there's no consistency as to how this is applied. Since publication is the only way in which other affected parties will find out about judgments that might offer them hope of recourse in their turn, this is plainly unsatisfactory.

For instance, in New Zealand the Insurance and Savings Ombudsman appears to be far more reluctant to publish findings than the Banking Ombudsman is. The contrast can be seen with the recent complaints against ANZ discussed in earlier chapters, where it is pretty well known that the Banking Ombudsman found in favour of complainants — and hence the office was swamped by other customers who have been similarly damaged. That's in direct contrast to a case involving a health insurer that changed the terms of the contract to all their clients from a fixed premium to an age-based premium. Clearly, all members were adversely affected, and I know of some who took complaints about this change to the Insurance and Savings Ombudsman and won. They were then bound by confidentiality, so the public at large were never really informed, and other affected parties remained unaware that they had potential recourse.

This patchiness is wrong, and the government should fix it. It suits the industry down to the ground to have complaints settled confidentially, because that way it can contain brush fires. But who cares what's in the interests of the corporates: it's the public interest that should be paramount. The powers of ombudsmen should be strengthened to compel them to publish all findings against companies where those findings have implications for other potential claimants. The consumer needs to know when an ombudsman has found wrongdoing by companies, so they too can make an informed choice about providers to whom they might give their business. It's just one of the ways in which the imbalance in information in this dysfunctional market can easily be corrected.

Swindlers list

The prevalence of out-and-out swindling by major enterprises has been extensive over recent years — Parmalat, Enron, Madoff, to name but a few. Fast-and-loose money, and the lack of prudential control over banks that is at the core of it, produces such blatant and, of course, illegal wrongdoing at the extremes. But you don't have to be breaking the law for your actions to be wrong, even if a rules-based regulatory regime tends to foster the opposite view. This is why changing to principles-based regulation is so important, so that participants in the economy know it is governed by a set of values that reflect the values held by wider society, and know that to step outside of these is to court society's sanction.

This simple morality has been lost in the maze of rules and regulations built up over decades. Government goons cannot hope to keep up with the slick operators in the private sector who easily game the system at the expense of simple fair play. That executives actually see arbitrage of rules, even where it performs a wrong upon someone else, as merely part of the rough-and-tumble of business, just tells us loudly and clearly how far we have departed as a society from the view that business should serve simply as a means of furthering economic well-being.

It's a sad state of affairs. But can we fix it?

11

Checklist for savers after the credit crisis

Time to summarise the messages in this book and compose some takeaways for those of you still interested.

Learn the rules of engagement

Bringing the curtain down on a decade or more of fast-and-loose credit was quick in the end — a long time coming, but quick and final. The issue for households is what will the world look like as the panic subsides? Do we just go back to business as usual, or will we have to adapt to an altogether different financial and economic environment? One thing is for sure — the global financial sector has already shrunk and will continue to do so. That's a damn good thing — as we saw in Chapter 4, this sector along with its obscene pay packets has inflicted a lot of damage on ordinary people and their savings, while central banks ignorantly abrogated all responsibility until their own credibility was laid to waste.

The first point to make is if you're contemplating putting money into the managed funds industry here, or if you're thinking of taking professional advice from a financial planner or advisor, your money is at risk. Because while I've spent a lot of the book talking about the macroeconomics of the present crisis (the big picture), it can't be allowed to divert attention away from the fact that the financial services industry both here and abroad is fundamentally sick. It's not that all players are — not by any means — but that far too many of those who solicit for people's savings just don't behave properly towards their clients. Just because an activity is legal doesn't mean it's right or ethical — and we have seen the abuse of fiduciary duty of care on a gross scale in recent years.

The macroeconomics is easy. The central banks allowed too much liquidity to flow into the world's financial system. Leave too much liquidity lying around and things will breed in it. In chapters 5 through 10, I put the pondlife of the New Zealand funds management and financial advisory industries under a microscope — yukkk! It's a cesspit!

In the aftermath of the collapse, policymakers the world over are at least aware of the infestation, and even made reassuring noises about addressing it — but they haven't done so yet. It's not unlike the situation of a homeowner who can't deal with the rats right now because the house is on fire. Most of the world's governments are just a little preoccupied at the moment, trying to prevent the global economy slipping into the abyss of depression. Some politicians are even clinging on to a dream that the good times will roll again as soon as central banks print enough money to overcome the problems of printing too much money, and governments have begun to spend themselves into a stupor.

Indeed, you couldn't be accused of undue cynicism if you suggested that policymakers have become so fixated on economic growth and so addicted to fast-and-loose credit that they'll let things continue as they are as the easy path back to those halcyon days, no matter how flawed that recipe has been shown to be.

So don't expect the financial sector to be rehabilitated any time soon. The worst of the institutions may be dead or dying but the ethical disease that leads them to abuse savers and investors is by no means cured. So if you mean to do business with it, you'll still need to wear white gumboots and breathing apparatus before handling their protestations of honesty, reliability, integrity and, above all, the insistence that they're in it to do you a service. Of course, insurance companies and some fund managers will argue all the way to oblivion that they're misunderstood, that they're the victim of a smear campaign and they're all Honest Joes and any lack of transparency around their procedures doesn't mean they're in the business of ripping people off.

Tell that to the thousands of victims in New Zealand of finance company and investment advisor incompetence or skulduggery. It is not about unfortunate market events: it's about financial product offerings that are misleading, opaque, and that benefit issuers directly at the expense of investors. Don't believe me? Look at what successive official enquiries have concluded about the ethics of this sector.

The 2005 Morris Review in the UK found the profession to be woefully corrupt. Nothing to do with us, you say? Well, the New Zealand government actuary testified to the Morris Review, and he had the following to say:

> While I was government actuary, with oversight of private pension schemes, I found trustees of a particular scheme were — in my view — endangering the security of benefits and misleading members in relation to a pension cash-out offer by relying on actuarial advice which I thought unprofessional. I accordingly laid a complaint of misconduct with the New Zealand Society of Actuaries.
>
> The NZSA took over two years to act on the complaint. The actuary concerned — a fellow of the Institute of Actuaries — took a litigious attitude . . .

And worse, he told the inquiry that he felt he was fighting an uphill battle, such was the level of undue influence that the industry had over policymakers:

> . . . in relation to the limited scrutiny I had of life insurance company operations, I came to the view that my professional reputation would be at some risk were I to continue under the existing conditions of work . . . examination of the submissions

made by the New Zealand actuarial profession to the New Zealand government shows that the concerns of the industries which employ actuaries are usually given greatest weight.

The recent (2009) review by Lord Turner (of Britain's Financial Services Authority) explained the 2008 credit crunch collapse thus:

> At the core of the crisis was an interplay between macroeconomic imbalances which have become particularly prevalent over the last 10–15 years, and financial market developments which have been going on for 30 years but which accelerated over the last ten under the influence of the macro imbalances.

In other words, too much fast-and-loose credit exacerbated the imbalances between borrowing and saving countries, and meanwhile the banking, insurance and financial service sectors went on a bit of a spree. Lord Turner noted that they indulged in

> . . . an economic rent extraction made possible by the opacity of margins and the asymmetry of information and knowledge between users of financial service and producers.

Finally, also from 2009, our own Registrar of Companies, speaking about local finance companies, noted that:

> the only objective of entering into one of these transactions [offering debentures to the public] was to benefit one of the directors (or interests associated with the director) or prop up a poor[ly] performing investment.

The bottom line is that the fiduciary duty of care by those charged with the guardianship of other people's money has been honoured only in the breach. It's a disease that originated in the life insurance industry and has spread across the global financial services sector to the extent that it is now 'normal' — 'standard international practice'.

But it's ethically and morally wrong and, combined with the lapse in central banks' maintenance of prudential supervision, has led to the collapse of the international financial system.

The good news is that it can be addressed easily if regulators can amass the collective intelligence to give prominence to principles of fair play in their rules, and to require financial service providers to have unlimited liability for any breach in their fiduciary duty. If, as the industry bleats continually — despite the most recent outbreak of unfettered swindling — it behaves properly anyway, then it won't have any problem providing the public with this additional reassurance, will it?

For trustees, administrators, managers and auditors of savings schemes, the implications of such a code of conduct are enormous. The supply of journeyman trustees will dry up overnight once they're burdened with unlimited exposure to the consequences of being party to wrongdoing. And so it should; many of these folk are little more than boardroom tourists, there for the sandwiches and the honorariums. Well-intentioned but financially illiterate trustees who are fully indemnified in law so long as they defer to their 'professional' advisors, are of no use to saver/investors whatsoever — especially not in a world where the financial advisory business is systemically corrupt and the regulator is comatose.

So for saver/investors going forward, until the day of principles-based regulation dawns and financial service providers are no longer allowed to walk away from their malpractice, it remains very much a case of buyer (or 'saver') beware. Treating everyone in the financial sector as a crook until proven otherwise seems to me the only prudent modus operandi.

So how does an advisor or provider prove to you they're well-intentioned? Two ways:

▷ By giving you, in writing, an assurance that they will maintain nothing less than a fiduciary duty of care over your assets, and that they will accept unlimited personal liability to you for any failure to achieve that standard. It's a simple undertaking. It wouldn't occupy more than a fraction of a percentage of the space wasted in most investment statements or statements of disclosure, but it would be worth more than all the rest put together. It would instantly separate the charlatans from the professional advisor.

▷ The second demand you should make is to ensure that you have sufficient transparency over what they're doing, so that you can independently validate their valuations and their account of transactions they've made with your money. Remember it is *your* money — even though the legal framework of superannuation schemes and unit trusts removes your legal ownership. Only if you can see through their units to what the underlying securities are can you run checks on them.

Unless you personally pursue these requirements — which should of course be statutory requirements if regulators weren't so lazy — you're little more than a lamb to the slaughter. And make no mistake, this sector will slaughter you with as little compunction as anyone wielding a big knife on the chain at the meatworks. Nor are these problems just the preserve of small, backstreet operators. The largest multinationals in the sector are actually very good at it and have more than enough resources to ensure you can't effectively challenge them in court.

That's the most pressing piece of advice in these troubled times. You have to take steps to protect yourself against the industry because waiting for the government to get around to reining it in is a luxury you can't afford.

Finally, on this stuff about protecting your back, I get asked by many who have had their savings destroyed by the practices prevalent in the savings and investment industry: 'How do we get justice?'

It's awful, really, but the reality is that your money is gone and you probably can't. The rotten moral standard of the industry and much of what we've seen happen in New Zealand are both legal. Ponzi schemes come about because the whole issue of misrepresentation is one of degree — the blatant lie of course is illegal (Madoff is in jail), but as we all know, in real life you can lie in effect by not telling your victim the whole truth; certainly not to the extent that they have the full facts to make an informed decision. Meet the financial sector — that's exactly how it works. Its rehabilitation is about people behaving properly — but don't get too excited about them making an early start.

Accountability is an important aspect of protecting the public interest and the purpose of the appendix of this book. But to the Mum and Dad who've been gutted by some in our financial establishment, I suggest you just stage a peaceful sit-in and demand your money back. That's your only recourse to justice — you'll feel better, perhaps, but your money will still be gone — pretty sick.

The New (Old) World of valuing assets

We hear a lot about the deleveraging of the world. That just means a smaller banking sector and far less credit flowing. But what does it mean for savers and their investments?

I'd suggest the biggest change will be to asset prices — without the steroids of central-bank neglect and the marked deterioration of credit quality that underwrites them, how will asset prices — and therefore investment returns — be determined? Let's finish the book with some fundamentals of investment to use in a world after the panic.

The return on an investment comprises two components — the year-by-year income the asset garners, and the change in the asset's price over the period you own it. For a company, that return is the sum of the after-tax profits and the change in value of the assets (buildings, plant and machinery, brand) that the company owns. For a shareholder, that return is the sum of the annual dividends and the change in the share price over the investment period. For a rental property it is the net rent plus the capital gain on the house.

Over the years of snowballing credit since the financial deregulation of the early 1980s, we've seen a rise in the proportion of returns that come from capital appreciation for many asset types and a fall in the relative contribution of dividends, rent or operating earnings.

Imagine for a moment a financial world in equilibrium, where economic growth and what contributes to it is perfectly foreseen. In that utopia of perfect foresight and zero imbalances (so no inflation, for example), we might expect all assets to be priced appropriately for risk (since there is no risk if we all have perfect foresight), and the total return each year for each asset to accrue solely from the income that asset earns. There would be little role for capital gains in this world, as all assets would be valued perfectly. Of course, the real world isn't like this, and it's the uncertainty and the surprises — the unforeseen business disasters and the surprise successes — that lead to capital gains, and the changing relative prices of assets. This is the point: capital gains or losses would normally accrue only to those assets when they surprise investors. In other words, capital gains or losses are a transitory component of the total return from an asset — not a permanent feature, year after year. The permanent feature ought to be the annual income. In the bubble economy from which we've just emerged, what we've been enjoying is far from this kind of reality.

Welcome to the New (Old) World — where asset prices reflect risk, where capital gains are the exception not the rule, where men are men and the women thankfully, are not. If this less-leveraged world is going to emerge and persist, then it's reasonable to expect asset prices to more accurately reflect the specific risks of that asset — that is, the risks specific to its future income. Restoration of adequate risk premiums between the earnings prospects of real-world assets and those 'risk-free' ones that governments offer on their bonds will see a return of the kind of asset price relativities that prevailed before the era of fast-and-loose credit. Let's see what that situation would look like.

The risk-free rate of investment is conventionally considered to be the yield on government bonds once inflation is netted out. In a world of large budget deficits such as we are entering, that will be around 3 per cent. You'll often hear this referred to as the 'real' interest rate. Now economic theory (and we won't have any more of that just now, thanks very much, so just believe me) tells us that this rate equals the average rate of economic growth. I'm guessing that growth at 2 per cent and allowing another 1 per cent for these massive government deficits that are coming to cover bailing the world out of its credit-crunch conundrum.

Each asset class will have to provide *risk premium* over and above the real, risk-free rate of 3 per cent. All we have to do is to assess what the risk premium is for each class of real (inflation-proofed) assets, in order to arrive at an *earnings yield* (or its commonly quoted inverse, the price-earnings, or P/E, ratio) norm for each asset class. Let's postulate what some 'normal' earnings yields will be.

Alignment of income yields

▷ **New Zealand shares:** This is a very small market, making it harder than usual to get in and out of shares, so I'd suggest a 4 per cent risk premium giving a normal (equilibrium or cyclically normal) earnings yield of 7 per cent, or a P/E of 14.

▷ **New Zealand rental property:** Similar to NZ shares, with less than perfect liquidity, but offering the owner much more direct control than shares do. This is appealing so warrants a lower risk premium on investment properties — let's say a premium of 3 per cent, so a net rental yield of 6 per cent (P/E of 17).

▷ **New Zealand farms:** Earnings are protected by the currency (if farm incomes are in trouble so is the whole economy, so important is this sector, so the currency will fall) which is a plus, and the owner has direct control too. But again, limited liquidity is a part-offset, so a risk premium of 3 per cent, giving a normal earnings yield of 6 per cent (P/E of 17).

▷ **International shares:** A risk premium of 3 per cent, but over the real bond rate for a stylised 'world bond' (the theoretical, international equivalent of the local risk-free rate for government bonds) which would be around 3 per cent (2 per cent world growth plus 1 per cent for big budget deficits) gives an equilibrium earnings yield of 6 per cent, or P/E of 17.

What does it all mean for the future of asset prices?
Now all of the above is just what someone might expect (in this case, me) to be normal P/E ratios prevailing in our less-leveraged world.

Of course, actual asset values will move above and below the so-called 'normal' valuations — markets, after all, over- and under-shoot as they search continuously for that elusive sustainable equilibrium. But the values importantly give us a guide and further, a basis for comparison of the New (Old) World with the one from whence we've come. What are the implications for asset prices?

▷ **International shares**: since financial deregulation of the 1980s, the average (historical earnings-based) P/E on the Standard & Poor's Index has been 21, though over the last 15 years (since Greenspan's 'irrational exuberance' speech), it has averaged 25. A return to a norm of 17 suggests a 30 per cent lower valuation for shares per dollar of earnings. This is certainly lower than we've recently become accustomed to.

▷ **New Zealand shares**: a normal or equilibrium P/E of 14 is lower than the 19 that we've become used to over the 1990s, so this is a downward re-rating in share values per dollar of earnings of about 25 per cent.

▷ **New Zealand rental property**: similarly, rental yields of around 4 per cent on commercial property and 3 per cent on residential have become de rigueur over recent decades, so 6 per cent on residential is a bit of a stink outlook, suggesting a 50 per cent fall in residential rental values per dollar of rental. Rental growth might provide some of that but it's hard to escape the prospect of a downward adjustment of house prices.

▷ **New Zealand farms**: again, an earnings yield on the average farm of 6 per cent as opposed to recent yields of 3 per cent is an awful prospect — unless, of course, earnings can be raised, a not altogether far-fetched notion given a lower currency.

Now, of course, the above are indicative only, conjectural even — feel free to try out your own numbers. But the message is clear — asset prices will be hurt in the absence of rises in income from those assets, as valuations resume a more rational and sustainable relativity to the risk-free rate. Without the fuel of fast-and-loose credit, the income return from assets becomes a far more important determinant of their capital value.

Property

In deference to Kiwis' passion for property, let's wrap up with a special mention of this asset class.

First, do you include property in a portfolio? Yes, of course. It's an important asset class. But to continue thinking of this as the single easiest way to get rich is nuts. New Zealand is in deep-debt doo-doo overseas, and the years of fast-and-loose credit have resulted in a meltdown — just in case you hadn't noticed. So in the current climate, our creditors are likely to be far more demanding on our banks when they lend them funds to loan to us. Higher deposit requirements are just one way in which the property market will be forced to adjust.

I retain the view that a serious adjustment in the *real* price of property (as shown earlier in Chapter 4 and repeated in the graph on the next page) is under way.

If full adjustment were to have occurred overnight from the mid-2007 peak, a 30 per cent fall would have been required. But two years on we now sit with real house prices down 12 per cent and still 20 per cent directly above the trendline — real prices have fallen 12 per cent and the sustainable trend value has lifted as well. If we were to fully close the gap with real prices falling at the rate they have been, then we'd be back on trend by mid-2010 (at Point A on the graph) with real house prices 25 per cent lower than they were at the 2007 peak (inflation causing an erosion of 11 per cent, actual house price falls accounting for the other 14 per cent).

But there's no guarantee whatsoever that's the way the adjustment will pan out, so let's consider a more sanguine alternative. Real house prices stagnate from now until enough time has passed for the long-

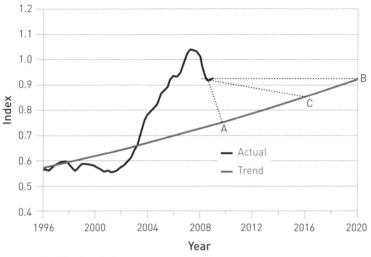

Real house prices

Source: Statistics New Zealand

term trend in house prices to 'catch up'. They'd be back in sync (at Point B on the graph) by 2019.

So which trajectory is it going to be? The answer is: I haven't really got a clue — but I could hazard a guess and I will in a minute. But suffice it to say that either way, housing isn't going to be a great investment for a while in our deleveraged world, as we're entering that era with houses valued well over historical trend (we talked in detail about that in Chapter 4).

I'd suggest a prudent pick would be to split the difference and allow five years for a full adjustment. If they're back on track by 2016 (Point C), then real house prices will have fallen by 20 per cent from their peak. On that scenario, the first two years (of the total seven-year adjustment) has seen price retreats that have already delivered over half of the total adjustment required (12 per cent), and the rest of it will take another five years over which roughly half of the adjustment comes from falling real house prices and half from a rising trend or equilibrium house price. In English, that means that over the next five years, assuming general inflation is say 3 per cent per annum, then house prices would only rise in total by about 7 per cent or just over 1 per cent per annum. Peace would reign.

Play with your own numbers, but the point is that house prices are still out of line. If you can't face it, then make like one of the few remaining land agents and pray for hordes of migrants to help out.

A final word

There will be life after the panic of 2008 — a panic that was a long time in the making and whose seeds were sown in the financial deregulation of 25 years ago, and then rolled and snowballed to a crescendo only a year ago. But it's not unreasonable to expect life to be very different — gone are the days where the profligate can keep spending other people's money, and nowhere is this more the case than in the financial products and services sector, which has been both the palace of excess and an abattoir for the savings of millions of people.

To expect the regulators to protect us all from our own vanity is to expect far too much. To expect them to lift the efficiency of regulation rather than the quantum of rules is perfectly reasonable. To expect central banks always to get it right is unrealistic. To expect them not to turn a blind eye to the madness of crowds is the least we should ask for. To expect governments to spend our way out is fanciful, although most are giving it a go.

In the end, as an economy we need to focus more readily on producing goods and services that people of the world want and are prepared to pay an amount that we can deliver them for. That's called sustainable growth. But then, if we decide to spend it all rather than save and invest, we will, in this deleveraged world, be pretty miserable. Yet if we save and have others allocate those savings ineffectively, we will also suffer.

After the panic of 2008, one can only hope that a more sober, less-leveraged attitude to economic activity prevails and that the widespread malfeasance of the finance sector is effectively brought to an end.

In the meantime, let the saver beware. This means you.

Appendix

Accountability — fundamental to well-functioning markets

The New Zealand financial sector has had its own meltdown over the last couple of years and there is a plethora of firms involved. Directors and trustees are directly responsible for the conduct of their companies or trusts, that is simply the law and one which investors need to be more conscious of when they make efforts to retrieve their funds. Put simply, it will not always be the case that directors are immune to legal redress personally because the company they were an official of, was a limited liability structure. It depends totally on the circumstances of the failure. Further, it's a sad fact that this sector has had its share of re-offenders - itself a tribute to the lack of effective regulatory control. And most commonly those that annihilated their clients' wealth have come back under different corporate guises. All too often, the public doesn't realise that it's dealing with someone who has wreaked such damage in the past.

There are some highly regarded New Zealanders on this list. I do not suggest that they are directly culpable, but as directors they are still responsible. If they weren't alert to what was going on at executive level then they were not fulfilling their directorial duties.

In chapters 8 and 9, I provided a sample of the incompetence that permeates the financial advisory and planning sector. There are hundreds of operators in that sector and the sample of deficient portfolios presented here is but the tip of the iceberg.

But as well as the advisors, of course, the sector has been infected with a profusion of toxic investments over recent years and behind each of these assets, too, lies more than an inert company name — there's a group of people responsible. From the investor's perspective, it is critical in my opinion that they have knowledge of who has demolished investor wealth in the past, so they can apply the 'once bitten, twice shy' principle to dealing with them in the future.

It's about accountability, and one of the major shortcomings of limited liability companies operating in the space where money from the public is invested is the ease with which those party to wealth destruction simply create a new company to practise again. The public needs a register to keep track of these operators.

Hopefully, the following record of who's been involved will help.

Table 1: Severely impaired or defunct companies and funds

Sources: The list of failed finance companies and funds is a matter of public record. The list of key people was taken from www.interest.co.nz

Hanover Finance

Date failed	July 2008
Current status	Moratorium
NZ$ at risk (m)	465
Number of clients	13,000
Key people	Mark Hotchin and Eric Watson
Activity of most public interest	Related-party transactions on non-commercial terms.

Bridgecorp

Date failed	July 2007
Current status	Receivership
NZ$ at risk (m)	459
Number of clients	18,000
Key people	Rod Petricevic
Activity of most public interest	Misleading information in prospectus.

OPI Pacific Finance (MFS Pacific Finance)

Date failed	March 2008
Current status	Liquidation
NZ$ at risk (m)	335
Number of clients	12,000
Key people	Jason Maywald
Activity of most public interest	Lent to related parties and lent an equal amount unsecured. The directors failed in their fiduciary duty of care to their clients.

Strategic Finance

Date failed	August 2008
Current status	Moratorium
NZ$ at risk (m)	330
Number of clients	15,000
Key people	Kerry Finnigan
Activity of most public interest	Funding mismatch with more than 80 per cent of its loans capitalising interest, so making the company extremely exposed to a property downturn. Some issues over quality of loan book.

Provincial Finance

Date failed	June 2006
Current status	Receivership
NZ$ at risk (m)	296
Number of clients	14,000
Key people	David Lyall
Activity of most public interest	Lent on used cars and many bad debts. Undercapitalised and at the lower end of the market. Poor management, weak balance sheets. All Black hard-man Colin 'Pinetree' Meads fronted the TV ads.

St Laurence

Date failed	June 2008
Current status	Moratorium
NZ$ at risk (m)	240
Number of clients	9000
Key people	Kevin Podmore
Activity of most public interest	Liquidity problems caused by low debenture reinvestment rates on one hand and late repayments from borrowers on the other — the classic borrow short and lend long.

Dominion Finance

Date failed	February 2009
Current status	Liquidation
NZ$ at risk (m)	224
Number of clients	6055
Key people	Terry Butler
Activity of most public interest	Lent significant amounts to related parties, 78 per cent of loan book in default with some of the dodgiest lending practices in the property development sector.

Capital + Merchant

Date failed	November 2007
Current status	Receivership
NZ$ at risk (m)	190
Number of clients	7000
Key people	Owen Tallentire
Activity of most public interest	mum-and-dad investors, many guided by financial planning firm Vestar, lost everything here. Undercapitalised and lent to related parties.

Dorchester

Date failed	June 2008
Current status	Moratorium
NZ$ at risk (m)	176
Number of clients	7800
Key people	Barry Graham
Activity of most public interest	Liquidity problems, lent long, borrowed short.

Nathans Finance

Date failed	August 2007
Current status	Receivership
NZ$ at risk (m)	174
Number of clients	7082
Key people	Gary Stevens
Activity of most public interest	Breached trust deed. Used an offshoot name so you thought they were around for much longer. Investors' funds went into thin air as 97 per cent of loan book went to related parties.

Geneva Finance

Date failed	October 2007
Current status	Moratorium
NZ$ at risk (m)	138
Number of clients	3000
Key people	Peter Francis
Activity of most public interest	Breached banking covenants.

Lombard Finance

Date failed	April 2008
Current status	Receivership
NZ$ at risk (m)	127
Number of clients	4400
Key people	Michael Reeves
Activity of most public interest	Lent long and borrowed short, failed due to the collapsing property market.

North South Finance

Date failed	June 2008
Current status	Moratorium
NZ$ at risk (m)	86
Number of clients	7
Key people	Terry Butler
Activity of most public interest	Loan book hit by write-downs and shared related loans with Dominion Finance.

Mascot Finance

Date failed	March 2009
Current status	Receivership
NZ$ at risk (m)	70
Number of clients	2558
Key people	Ken Lane
Activity of most public interest	None.

United Finance

Date failed	July 2008
Current status	Moratorium
NZ$ at risk (m)	65
Number of clients	2400
Key people	Mark Hotchin and Eric Watson
Activity of most public interest	Related to the Hanover Group.

Five Star Consumer Finance

Date failed	August 2007
Current status	Receivership
NZ$ at risk (m)	51
Number of clients	2145
Key people	Anthony Bowden
Activity of most public interest	Related-party loans as well as high-value, complex loans that appear to be outside of normal commercial lending practices.

Orange Finance

Date failed	December 2008
Current status	Suspended
NZ$ at risk (m)	50
Number of clients	2500
Key people	Doug Somers-Edgar
Activity of most public interest	Raised finance through Money Managers founded by Doug Somers-Edgar.

Western Bay Finance

Date failed	July 2006
Current status	Receivership
NZ$ at risk (m)	48
Number of clients	2500
Key people	Jim Smylie
Activity of most public interest	Undercapitalised and at the lower end of the market. Poor management, weak balance sheets.

Boston Finance

Date failed	March 2008
Current status	Moratorium
NZ$ at risk (m)	40
Number of clients	1500
Key people	Jason Maywald
Activity of most public interest	Related to Vestar and MFS.

National Finance 2000

Date failed	May 2006
Current status	Receivership
NZ$ at risk (m)	25
Number of clients	2026
Key people	Allan Ludlow
Activity of most public interest	Reckless trading; failure to comply with prospectus; breach of director's duties; related-party transactions and failure to maintain adequate books and records.

Beneficial Finance

Date failed	October 2007
Current status	Moratorium
NZ$ at risk (m)	24
Number of clients	750
Key people	Mervyn Oldham
Activity of most public interest	None.

Hanover Capital

Date failed	July 2008
Current status	Moratorium
NZ$ at risk (m)	24
Number of clients	1100
Key people	Mark Hotchin and Eric Watson
Activity of most public interest	Related-party transactions on non-commercial terms.

Belgrave Finance

Date failed	May 2008
Current status	Receivership
NZ$ at risk (m)	20
Number of clients	1000
Key people	Steve Smith
Activity of most public interest	Failed to find new funding, but also noted poor lending standards and book-keeping.

Compass Capital

Date failed	March 2009
Current status	Receivership
NZ$ at risk (m)	20
Number of clients	800
Key people	Ian Gladwell
Activity of most public interest	Formerly linked to Bridgecorp as an offshoot.

LDC Finance

Date failed	September 2007
Current status	Receivership
NZ$ at risk (m)	19
Number of clients	995
Key people	Murray Scholfield
Activity of most public interest	None.

Chancery Finance

Date failed	August 2007
Current status	Receivership
NZ$ at risk (m)	18
Number of clients	1374
Key people	Gary Stevens
Activity of most public interest	Related-party transactions on non-commercial terms.

Finance & Investments

Date failed	September 2007
Current status	Receivership
NZ$ at risk (m)	16
Number of clients	370
Key people	Murray Scholfield
Activity of most public interest	None.

Clegg & Co

Date failed	October 2007
Current status	Receivership
NZ$ at risk (m)	15
Number of clients	496
Key people	Brian Clegg
Activity of most public interest	Related-party transactions and problems are thought to have long predated receivership.

Cymbis NZ (Fairview)

Date failed	May 2008
Current status	Receivership
NZ$ at risk (m)	7
Number of clients	797
Key people	Owen Tallentire
Activity of most public interest	Member of the collapsed Capital + Merchant Group and changed name to Fairview — wonder why?

St Kilda Finance

Date failed	August 2008
Current status	Receivership
NZ$ at risk (m)	7
Number of clients	358
Key people	John Farry
Activity of most public interest	None — deteriorating trading conditions.

Numeria Finance

Date failed	December 2007
Current status	Receivership
NZ$ at risk (m)	7
Number of clients	480
Key people	Owen Tallentire
Activity of most public interest	None.

Antares

Date failed	August 2007
Current status	Receivership
NZ$ at risk (m)	3
Number of clients	100
Key people	Anthony Bowden
Activity of most public interest	None.

Kiwi Finance

Date failed	April 2008
Current status	Receivership
NZ$ at risk (m)	2
Number of clients	42
Key people	Rod Greensill
Activity of most public interest	None.

Table 2: Companies & funds with a liquidity crisis

Sources: The data comes from www.interest.co.nz and information in the 'Activity of most public interest' from media articles on each specific business failure.

ING Diversified Yield Fund

Date failed	March 2008
Current status	Suspended
NZ$ at risk (m)	427
Number of clients	4000
Activity of most public interest	Inappropriately promoted by ANZ and others as low- to medium-risk investment that will achieve an investment yield of 10 per cent gross pa. 2005 annual report suggested that 81 per cent of this fund was invested in CDOs.

ING Regular Income Fund

Date failed	March 2008
Current status	Suspended
NZ$ at risk (m)	232
Number of clients	2000
Activity of most public interest	Inappropriately promoted by ANZ and others as low to medium risk designed to provide regular income and as an alternative to short-term bank deposits and finance company debentures by investing in CDOs.

ING Enhanced Yield Fund

Date failed	December 2008
Current status	Closed
NZ$ at risk (m)	27
Number of clients	417
Activity of most public interest	Promoted as a low- to medium-risk investment to provide a consistent and stable return above the cash rate by investing in hybrid securities, credit derivatives and structured fixed-interest securities.

ING Credit Opportunities Fund

Date failed	December 2008
Current status	Closed
NZ$ at risk (m)	8
Number of clients	294
Activity of most public interest	Medium- to high-risk fund that invests in CDOs, CDSs (credit default swaps), derivatives and other securities aiming for absolute or total returns. As at 31/03/09 the performance was -60.92 per cent.

ING Diversified Trading Fund — PPS

Date failed	January 2009
Current status	Closed
NZ$ at risk (m)	6
Number of clients	?
Activity of most public interest	Maximise capital growth while preserving capital through investing in primarily one or more absolute return funds.

AMP NZ Property Fund

Date failed	August 2008
Current status	Suspended
NZ$ at risk (m)	419
Number of clients	2900
Activity of most public interest	Allows liquidity in an investment product that has highly illiquid assets as the major investment – simply ran out of liquidity.

Canterbury Mortgage Trust

Date failed	July 2008
Current status	Closed
NZ$ at risk (m)	250
Number of clients	5000
Activity of most public interest	Lent long, borrowed short, high rate of loan arrears.

Guardian Mortgage Fund

Date failed	July 2008
Current status	Closed
NZ$ at risk (m)	249
Number of clients	3700
Activity of most public interest	Liquidity problem due to property market.

Tower Mortgage Fund

Date failed	April 2008
Current status	Closed
NZ$ at risk (m)	242
Number of clients	5000
Activity of most public interest	Liquidity problem due to property market.

AXA Mortgage Fund

Date failed	October 2008
Current status	Suspended
NZ$ at risk (m)	225
Number of clients	5000
Activity of most public interest	Liquidity problem due to property market.

AXA Mortgage Bonds

Date failed	August 2008
Current status	Closed
NZ$ at risk (m)	17
Number of clients	901
Activity of most public interest	Liquidity problem due to property market.

IMP Diversified Fund

Date failed	June 2008
Current status	Moratorium
NZ$ at risk (m)	16
Number of clients	1015
Activity of most public interest	Market related.

Table 3: Directory of directors

Sources: The list of directors comes directly from the New Zealand Companies Office.

ARKINSTALL, Vance Eric

Date appointed	8 November 2003
Date resigned	
Date of company failure	2 June 2008
Company	**Dominion Finance**

ARKINSTALL, Vance Eric

Date appointed	12 April 2006
Date resigned	
Date of company failure	June 2008
Company	**North South Finance Ltd**

AVERILL, Colin Ernest Walter

Date appointed	30 April 2004
Date resigned	20 December 2007
Date of company failure	June 2006
Company	**Provincial Finance Ltd**

BANBROOK, Anthony David

Date appointed	27 March 2002
Date resigned	
Date of company failure	May 2006
Company	**National Finance 2000**

BELLAS, Mark Theodore

Date appointed	16 November 2005
Date resigned	24 September 2007
Date of company failure	August 2007
Company	**PropertyFinance Securities**

BETTLE, Richard Gilbert

Date appointed	24 March 2004
Date resigned	
Date of company failure	June 2008
Company	**Dominion Finance**

BETTLE, Richard Gilbert

Date appointed	31 March 2006
Date resigned	
Date of company failure	June 2008
Company	**North South Finance Ltd**

BOWDEN, Anthony Walpole

Date appointed	23 November 2005
Date resigned	
Date of company failure	August 2007
Company	**Antares Finance Holdings Ltd**

BOWDEN, Anthony Walpole

Date appointed	2 April 2001
Date resigned	
Date of company failure	August 2007
Company	**Five Star Consumer Finance**

BRAITHWAITE, Carol Anne

Date appointed	4 April 2000
Date resigned	
Date of company failure	May 2006
Company	**National Finance 2000**

BRYANT, Lawrence Roland Valpy

Date appointed	11 October 2002
Date resigned	
Date of company failure	April 2008
Company	**Lombard Finance & Investments**

BUCKLEY, Shane Joseph

Date appointed	30 August 2005
Date resigned	
Date of company failure	May 2008
Company	**Belgrave Finance Ltd**

BUTLER, Ann Kathleen

Date appointed	31 March 2006
Date resigned	12 November 2008
Date of company failure	June 2008
Company	**North South Finance Ltd**

BUTLER, Ann Kathleen

Date appointed	7 November 2001
Date resigned	
Date of company failure	June 2008
Company	**Dominion Finance**

BUTLER, Hayden Stuart

Date appointed	8 November 2003
Date resigned	
Date of company failure	June 2008
Company	**Dominion Finance**

BUTLER, Terence Maxwell

Date appointed	31 March 2006
Date resigned	12 November 2008
Date of company failure	June 2008
Company	**North South Finance Ltd**

BUTLER, Terence Maxwell

Date appointed	7 November 2001
Date resigned	
Date of company failure	June 2008
Company	**Dominion Finance**

BYRNES, Paul Anthony

Date appointed	2 February 2004
Date resigned	
Date of company failure	June 2008
Company	**Dorchester Finance Ltd**

CLEGG, Brian Samuel

Date appointed	26 March 2004
Date resigned	
Date of company failure	October 2007
Company	**Clegg & Co Finance Ltd**

DAVIDSON, Bruce Nelson

Date appointed	30 April 2001
Date resigned	
Date of company failure	July 2007
Company	**Bridgecorp Ltd**

DAVIS, Leigh Robert

Date appointed	16 November 2005
Date resigned	24 September 2007
Date of company failure	August 2007
Company	**PropertyFinance Securities**

EDILSON, John Simon

Date appointed	9 December 1997
Date resigned	
Date of company failure	June 2006
Company	**Provincial Finance Ltd**

ELLIOTT, Kevin

Date appointed	5 February 2004
Date resigned	
Date of company failure	September 2007
Company	**LDC Finance Ltd**

FARRY, John Edward

Date appointed	10 April 2003
Date resigned	
Date of company failure	September 2007
Company	**St Kilda Finance (All Purpose Finance)**

FINNIGAN, Kerry

Date appointed	1 November 2005
Date resigned	
Date of company failure	August 2008
Company	**Strategic Finance Ltd**

FISHER, Michael John

Date appointed	19 December 2006
Date resigned	
Date of company failure	June 2008
Company	**Dorchester Finance Ltd**

FORSYTH, Paul Winstone

Date appointed	8 November 2003
Date resigned	
Date of company failure	June 2008
Company	**Dominion Finance**

FRANCIS, Peter Edward

Date appointed	19 August 2002
Date resigned	
Date of company failure	October 2007
Company	**Geneva Finance**

GLADWELL, Ian Wayne

Date appointed	13 July 2007
Date resigned	
Date of company failure	August 2008
Company	**Compass Capital Ltd**

GORDON, Bruce Patrick

Date appointed	5 December 2007
Date resigned	30 October 2008
Date of company failure	July 2008
Company	**Hanover Capital Ltd**

GORDON, Bruce Patrick

Date appointed	5 December 2007
Date resigned	30 October 2008
Date of company failure	July 2008
Company	**Hanover Finance Ltd**

GORDON, Bruce Patrick

Date appointed	5 December 2007
Date resigned	30 October 2008
Date of company failure	July 2008
Company	**United Finance Ltd**

GOSNEY, John James

Date appointed	28 May 2008
Date resigned	
Date of company failure	June 2008
Company	**Dorchester Finance Ltd**

GRAHAM, Barry Walter John

Date appointed	27 September 1996
Date resigned	
Date of company failure	June 2008
Company	**Dorchester Finance Ltd**

GRAHAM, Sir Douglas Arthur Montrose

Date appointed	11 October 2002
Date resigned	
Date of company failure	April 2008
Company	**Lombard Finance & Investments**

GREEN, Adrian Lance

Date appointed	25 March 2004
Date resigned	
Date of company failure	March 2008
Company	**Boston Finance Ltd**

GREENSILL, Rodney Seymour Roberts

Date appointed	13 December 2005
Date resigned	
Date of company failure	April 2008
Company	**Kiwi Finance**

HARDIMAN, Christopher John

Date appointed	5 February 2004
Date resigned	
Date of company failure	September 2007
Company	**LDC Finance Ltd**

HAZLETT, Denis Luke

Date appointed	14 March 2002
Date resigned	24 September 2007
Date of company failure	August 2007
Company	**PropertyFinance Securities**

HILL, Stephen Frank

Date appointed	20 January 2005
Date resigned	31 March 2008
Date of company failure	March 2008
Company	**Boston Finance Ltd**

HOBBS, Michael James Bowie

Date appointed	15 August 2000
Date resigned	
Date of company failure	August 2008
Company	**Strategic Finance Ltd**

HOTCHIN, John

Date appointed	23 July 2001
Date resigned	15 April 2007
Date of company failure	August 2007
Company	**Nathans Finance NZ Ltd**

HOTCHIN, Mark Stephen

Date appointed	4 August 2005
Date resigned	
Date of company failure	July 2008
Company	**Hanover Capital Ltd**

HOTCHIN, Mark Stephen

Date appointed	24 December 1999
Date resigned	
Date of company failure	July 2008
Company	**Hanover Finance Ltd**

HOTCHIN, Mark Stephen

Date appointed	10 August 2004
Date resigned	
Date of company failure	July 2008
Company	**United Finance Ltd**

HUTCHISON, Peter James

Date appointed	7 February 2003
Date resigned	
Date of company failure	August 2008
Company	**St Kilda Finance (All Purpose Finance)**

JACKSON, Graham Edward

Date appointed	4 April 2002
Date resigned	
Date of company failure	August 2008
Company	**Strategic Finance Ltd**

JANNETTO, John Charles

Date appointed	16 December 2004
Date resigned	21 March 2008
Date of company failure	September 2007
Company	**LDC Finance Ltd**

JEFFRIES, The Hon William Patrick

Date appointed	11 October 2002
Date resigned	
Date of company failure	April 2008
Company	**Lombard Finance & Investments**

JOHNSTON, Donald Howard

Date appointed	10 November 1997
Date resigned	
Date of company failure	July 2006
Company	**Western Bay Finance Ltd**

KIRK, Nicholas George

Date appointed	23 November 2005
Date resigned	
Date of company failure	August 2007
Company	**Antares Finance Holdings Ltd**

KIRK, Nicholas George

Date appointed	2 October 1998
Date resigned	
Date of company failure	August 2007
Company	**Five Star Consumer Finance**

LAMBERT, Barry Noel

Date appointed	10 May 2007
Date resigned	
Date of company failure	April 2008
Company	**Kiwi Finance**

LINDALE, Marc Aubrey

Date appointed	1 December 2000
Date resigned	
Date of company failure	August 2008
Company	**Strategic Finance Ltd**

LUDLOW, Trevor Allan

Date appointed	6 September 1999
Date resigned	
Date of company failure	May 2006
Company	**National Finance 2000**

LYALL, David Robert

Date appointed	24 Feburary 1993
Date resigned	30 November 2006
Date of company failure	June 2006
Company	**Provincial Finance Ltd**

MACDONALD, Marcus Arthur

Date appointed	23 November 2005
Date resigned	
Date of company failure	August 2007
Company	**Antares Finance Holdings Ltd**

MACDONALD, Marcus Arthur

Date appointed	2 October 1998
Date resigned	
Date of company failure	August 2007
Company	**Five Star Consumer Finance**

MAHER, Andrew John

Date appointed	18 June 2004
Date resigned	29 April 2008
Date of company failure	October 2007
Company	**Clegg & Co Finance Ltd**

MATSON, Oliver Roderick

Date appointed	19 August 2003
Date resigned	
Date of company failure	August 2008
Company	**St Kilda Finance (All Purpose Finance)**

MAYWALD, Jason

Date appointed	
Date resigned	
Date of company failure	March 2008
Company	**MFS Pacific Finance**

MILLER, David Gordon

Date appointed	5 February 2004
Date resigned	
Date of company failure	September 2007
Company	**LDC Finance Ltd**

MOODY, Robert John

Date appointed	12 May 2006
Date resigned	
Date of company failure	August 2008
Company	**Compass Capital Ltd**

MOSES, Kenneth Roger

Date appointed	11 August 2003
Date resigned	
Date of company failure	August 2007
Company	**Nathans Finance NZ Ltd**

MUIR, Gregory John

Date appointed	22 February 2006
Date resigned	1 April 2009
Date of company failure	July 2008
Company	**Hanover Capital Ltd**

MUIR, Gregory John

Date appointed	22 February 2006
Date resigned	1 April 2009
Date of company failure	July 2008
Company	**Hanover Finance Ltd**

MUIR, Gregory John

Date appointed	22 February 2006
Date resigned	1 April 2009
Date of company failure	July 2008
Company	**United Finance Ltd**

NICHOLLS, Neal Medhurst

Date appointed	31 March 2006
Date resigned	
Date of company failure	November 2007
Company	**Capital + Merchant Finance**

NICHOLLS, Neal Medhurst

Date appointed	3 June 2005
Date resigned	
Date of company failure	November 2007
Company	**Capital + Merchant Investments Ltd**

NICHOLLS, Neal Medhurst

Date appointed   31 January 2007
Date resigned
Date of company failure   December 2007
Company   **Numeria Finance**

O'CONNELL, David Gerard

Date appointed   19 June 2007
Date resigned
Date of company failure   October 2007
Company   **Geneva Finance**

OLDHAM, Kane Edward

Date appointed   21 November 2003
Date resigned
Date of company failure   October 2007
Company   **Beneficial Finance**

OLDHAM, Mervyn John

Date appointed   25 September 1989
Date resigned
Date of company failure   October 2007
Company   **Beneficial Finance**

OLDHAM, Simon Craig

Date appointed   12 February 1997
Date resigned
Date of company failure   October 2007
Company   **Beneficial Finance**

O'REGAN, Sir Tipene Gerard

Date appointed   4 August 2005
Date resigned   30 October 2008
Date of company failure   July 2008
Company   **Hanover Capital Ltd**

O'REGAN, Sir Tipene Gerard

Date appointed   18 August 2004
Date resigned   30 October 2008
Date of company failure   July 2008
Company   **Hanover Finance Ltd**

O'REGAN, Sir Tipene Gerard

Date appointed	18 August 2004
Date resigned	30 October 2008
Date of company failure	July 2008
Company	**United Finance Ltd**

O'SULLIVAN, Aeneas Edward

Date appointed	13 June 2005
Date resigned	
Date of company failure	June 2008
Company	**St Laurence Finance Ltd**

PERRY, Stuart Alexander Mccrae

Date appointed	19 August 2003
Date resigned	
Date of company failure	August 2008
Company	**St Kilda Finance (All Purpose Finance)**

PETRICEVIC, Rodney Michael

Date appointed	30 April 2001
Date resigned	
Date of company failure	July 2007
Company	**Bridgecorp Ltd**

PODMORE, Kevin John

Date appointed	13 June 2005
Date resigned	
Date of company failure	June 2008
Company	**St Laurence Finance Ltd**

QUEEN, Darryl Bruce

Date appointed	1 May 2001
Date resigned	
Date of company failure	August 2007
Company	**PropertyFinance Securities**

REEVES, Michael Howard

Date appointed	17 December 2002
Date resigned	
Date of company failure	April 2008
Company	**Lombard Finance & Investments**

RICH, Timothy John

Date appointed	21 March 2006
Date resigned	21 October 2008
Date of company failure	August 2008
Company	**Strategic Finance Ltd**

RILEY, Shaun Lee

Date appointed	19 June 2007
Date resigned	21 December 2007
Date of company failure	October 2007
Company	**Geneva Finance**

ROEST, Cornelis Robert

Date appointed	17 July 2006
Date resigned	
Date of company failure	July 2007
Company	**Bridgecorp Ltd**

RYAN, Colin Gregory

Date appointed	19 December 2006
Date resigned	
Date of company failure	October 2007
Company	**Capital + Merchant Finance**

RYAN, Colin Gregory

Date appointed	25 January 2007
Date resigned	26 November 2007
Date of company failure	May 2008
Company	**Cymbis NZ**

SMITH, Stephen Charles

Date appointed	30 August 2005
Date resigned	
Date of company failure	May 2008
Company	**Belgrave Finance Ltd**

SMYLIE, James Lindsay

Date appointed	20 June 1989
Date resigned	
Date of company failure	July 2006
Company	**Western Bay Finance Ltd**

SMYLIE, Kaaren Ilse

Date appointed	8 December 2003
Date resigned	
Date of company failure	July 2006
Company	**Western Bay Finance Ltd**

SOMERS-EDGAR, Douglas Lloyd

Date appointed	3 July 2003
Date resigned	
Date of company failure	December 2008
Company	**Orange Finance Ltd**

STEIGRAD, Peter David

Date appointed	23 May 2003
Date resigned	
Date of company failure	July 2007
Company	**Bridgecorp Ltd**

STEIN, Wendy Joan

Date appointed	19 August 2003
Date resigned	
Date of company failure	August 2008
Company	**St Kilda Finance (All Purpose Finance)**

STEVENS, Gary James

Date appointed	29 March 2004
Date resigned	
Date of company failure	August 2007
Company	**Chancery Finance**

SUNDSTRUM, Barnaby Innes

Date appointed	1 May 2001
Date resigned	
Date of company failure	August 2007
Company	**PropertyFinance Securities**

SUTHERLAND, Robert Gordon

Date appointed	30 November 2006
Date resigned	
Date of company failure	November 2007
Company	**Capital + Merchant Finance**

SUTHERLAND, Robert Gordon
Date appointed	25 January 2007
Date resigned	4 December 2007
Date of company failure	May 2008
Company	**Cymbis NZ**

TALLENTIRE, Owen Francis
Date appointed	12 October 2006
Date resigned	
Date of company failure	November 2007
Company	**Capital + Merchant Finance**

TALLENTIRE, Owen Francis
Date appointed	12 October 2006
Date resigned	
Date of company failure	November 2007
Company	**Capital + Merchant Investments Ltd**

TALLENTIRE, Owen Francis
Date appointed	25 January 2007
Date resigned	
Date of company failure	May 2008
Company	**Cymbis NZ**

TALLENTIRE, Owen Francis
Date appointed	12 October 2006
Date resigned	
Date of company failure	December 2007
Company	**Numeria Finance**

TAYLOR, Peter John Morgan
Date appointed	5 February 2004
Date resigned	24 September 2007
Date of company failure	August 2007
Company	**PropertyFinance Securities**

THOM, Denis Grenville
Date appointed	7 September 2001
Date resigned	
Date of company failure	August 2008
Company	**Strategic Finance Ltd**

TURNER, Stephen Kingsley Edgar

Date appointed	25 March 2004
Date resigned	
Date of company failure	March 2008
Company	**Boston Finance Ltd**

URWIN, Gary Kenneth

Date appointed	23 May 2003
Date resigned	
Date of company failure	July 2007
Company	**Bridgecorp Ltd**

WALKER, Glenn Andrew

Date appointed	19 August 2002
Date resigned	18 April 2008
Date of company failure	October 2007
Company	**Geneva Finance**

WALSH, Brian

Date appointed	20 September 2003
Date resigned	
Date of company failure	October 2007
Company	**Geneva Finance**

WHALE, Robert Barry

Date appointed	31 March 2006
Date resigned	10 September 2008
Date of company failure	June 2008
Company	**North South Finance Ltd**

WHALE, Robert Barry

Date appointed	8 November 2003
Date resigned	
Date of company failure	June 2008
Company	**Dominion Finance**

WHEELER, Philip Brent

Date appointed	1 December 2005
Date resigned	
Date of company failure	June 2006
Company	**Provincial Finance Ltd**

WOLFENDEN, David John

Date appointed	7 September 2001
Date resigned	
Date of company failure	August 2008
Company	**Strategic Finance Ltd**

YATES, Samantha Lee

Date appointed	21 November 2003
Date resigned	19 May 2009
Date of company failure	October 2007
Company	**Beneficial Finance**

YOUNG, Donald Menzies

Date appointed	12 September 2005
Date resigned	
Date of company failure	August 2007
Company	**Nathans Finance NZ Ltd**

Table 4: Veritable quotes from officials of malfunctioning firms

Sources: As indicated

Provincial Finance Limited

Source Prospectus 2005

Quote You can have peace of mind when investing with Provincial Finance as you're dealing with an experienced, dedicated finance company . . . More than 14,500 New Zealanders trust Provincial Finance with their hard earned money. Like them, when you invest with Provincial Finance you'll enjoy high levels of personal service, regular, easy to understand performance reports, attention to risk, and a good rate of return over the term of your investment.

Beneficial Finance

Source Prospectus 2006

Quote Beneficial Finance undertakes lending and investing activities . . . Beneficial Finance has many years of experience in dealing with this market and has established systems in place to recover monies lent to such individuals.

The company has a credit policy, which is used to manage its exposure to credit risk. As part of this policy credit evaluations are performed on all prospective borrowers, limits on exposures set, and lending is subject to defined criteria and is monitored and controlled by prudent credit measures.

After considering its current portfolio Beneficial Finance is comfortable with its risk profile as at the date of this prospectus (22-09-06).

Lombard

Source Annual report 2006

Quote Our governance and management team brings together considerable experience in the various disciplines required to effectively manage the funds you have entrusted to us. Our investment philosophy aligns performance and risk management considerations.

Numeria

Source Advertorial

Quote Our name, derived from the Latin word for finance, reflects our reliance on conservative financial practices and focus on steady growth.

. . . sectors deemed as high risk will be avoided. The company is dedicated to conservative lending fundamentals.

Geneva

Source Prospectus May 2008

Quote Geneva now has a conservative equity ratio, and committed funding lines over the next three years . . . Geneva is now better equipped to identify and react more effectively to market changes, so as to maximise the company's profitability.

Nathans Finance

Source Prospectus 2006

Quote At Nathans, our team of dedicated finance professionals have two core objectives: (1) To provide our investors with attractive interest rates; (2) Peace of mind by offering quality finance solutions to businesses and individuals that meet Nathans' prudential lending requirements in line with the Company's Credit Policy. Nathans does not lend into the 'higher risk' consumer areas such as vehicle and retail consumer lending. Nathans' consistent profits combined with robust credit assessment process and a strong level of corporate governance have ensured that we have retained our unblemished record of nil bad debts written off for the period ending 30 June 2006.

Antares

Source Prospectus 2006

Quote As a director of Antares Finance Holdings Limited, I would like to recommend to you this issue of fully-voting ordinary shares . . . The board believes that the shares offer good investment value and will be of interest to those investors who are looking to maximise their investment return and growth in good quality securities.
(In letter from Marcus Macdonald, chairman of directors.)

Clegg & Co Finance

Source Prospectus August 2006

Quote At a time when the finance industry is under renewed scrutiny from the authorities and the public alike, directors have assured that this growth (of company in past year) has been accompanied by a strengthening of the company's management team and continued attention to a conservative credit policy and lending criteria. Clegg & Co remains a family owned firm committed to a conservative lending policy for the protection and in the mutual interest of depositors and shareholders.

Capital + Merchant Finance

Source Prospectus 2007

Quote Capital + Merchant Finance is of the opinion that it has 'insured' itself in the unlikely event that there was to be a loss on some or a number of its investments. The Company carries a cash reserve to cover fluctuations of investments and lending.

Boston Finance

Source Prospectus September 2007

Quote MFS Boston aims to provide investors in the Secured Debenture Stock with a competitive return on their investment while conducting its lending operations in a prudent manner.

Cymbis

Source   Mortage 50 fund product disclosure statement 10 March 2008

Quote   We believe that the Fund is based on very conservative coverage and that such conservative coverage sets us apart from many of our competitors. We consider our security coverage to be conservative because our investors are provided with added protection and first loss provision as moneys lent to a borrower from funds raised are insured under mortgage indemnity insurance and mortgage impairment insurance policies underwritten by certain syndicates of Lloyd's of London.

Belgrave Finance

Source   Prospectus October 2007

Quote   After due inquiry by the directors in relation to the period between 31 March 2007 and the date of registration of this Prospectus, the directors are of the opinion that no circumstances have arisen which would materially adversely affect the trading or profitability of Belgrave Finance Ltd or the value of its assets or the ability of Belgrave Finance Ltd to pay its liabilities due within the next 12 months.
(signed by Shane Buckley and Stephen Smith – directors)

North South Finance

Source   Prospectus September 2007

Quote   NSFL's directors have experienced a number of economic downturns and have the requisite experience to protect our shareholder funds and our Investors' funds.

Canterbury Mortgage Trust

Source   www.cmt.co.nz

Quote   Canterbury Mortgage Trust provides managed mortgage investments and mortgage finance throughout New Zealand. The Fund aims to provide investors with a low risk investment . . . and therefore achieve benefits that may not be possible individually.

IMP Diversified Income Fund

Source   Prospectus November 2008

Quote   Notwithstanding the difficult market conditions that currently prevail, a number of factors make IMP better off than many others in the industry: (1) IMP invests in businesses rather than property developers and individuals, and consequently has a very different risk profile to other industry participants. This helps IMP investors to better diversify their investment portfolio and in turn provides IMP with a true competitive advantage vis-a-vis other Debenture Stock issuers; (2) IMP has a greater proportion of equity on the Balance Sheet relative to others in the industry providing IMP with the financial reliance to withstand some of these market conditions; and (3) IMP is well supported by a number of large financial advisory firms. These factors will help 'weather the storm' in the short term before the market stabilises.

St Laurence

Source Investment statement April 2006

Quote St Laurence has considerable experience in mortgage lending, property management, property investment, property development and funds management. This combination of skills puts St Laurence in a strong position of being able to source and review transactions using a coordinated and multi-disciplined approach . . . Under this offer investors have the opportunity to become Shareholders in the Company and holders of Bonds issued by the Company. As an investor you will participate in the potential growth of the Company, yet at the same time benefit from a fixed interest return through the ownership of Bonds.

Dorchester

Source Prospectus December 2007

Quote Dorchester Finance maintains a spread of risk through a lending policy that ensures a spread of loans across a number of industries and also throughout New Zealand and by having a Lending and Credit Committee of the Board of Directors of its parent, NZX listed Dorchester Pacific Limited oversee its lending activities.

Hanover Finance

Source Prospectus December 2007

Quote Central to our business strategy is an understanding of the importance of prudent cash management. It is also important to maintain a balance between maturities of loans to borrowers on one hand, and funding from investors on the other, in order to ensure that investors are paid in full when their Secured Deposits mature. Our investors can take comfort that we are well placed in these areas.

Hanover Capital

Source Prospectus December 2007

Quote We believe the wealth of experience and strong governance structures differentiates Hanover Finance from others in the sector.

Hanover Finance has finished the year in a very sound financial position . . . They are well placed to continue to deliver good returns to their investors. Hanover Finance has managed through demanding market conditions before and believes this focus on prudent management is paramount . . . With this approach, even when current market conditions are considered the board is confident of Hanover Finance's ability to continue to meet its obligations to the Company and other investors as they fall due.

United Finance

Source   Prospectus December 2007

Quote   Central to our business strategy is an understanding of the importance of prudent cash management.

The Board of United Finance anticipates operating conditions in the year ahead will be more challenging than in the previous 12 months. However, we believe that our cash management strategies will enable us to continue to deliver good returns to our investors.

Guardian Mortgage

Source   Fund description 2008

Quote   An income fund investing in low-risk quality first mortgages.

Strategic Finance

Source   Annual Report 2007

Quote   This board has insisted that at all times the Company remains focused on best business practice principles applying astute financial judgement, both in running our own business and in choosing where and how we invest. (Denis Thom, chairman)

Our well capitalised balance sheet, our cash on hand and our potential to access capital means that Strategic Finance will be well positioned for a strong result for the 2007/08 financial year. Importantly our diverse property lending portfolio gives us a good position to manage the short term challenge of a possible slowdown in growth in property investment. (Kerry Finnigan, CEO)

Orange Finance

Source   Investment Statement September 2006

Quote   Created by professionals with many years experience in the financial services industry. 'I am delighted to offer you the opportunity to invest in a First Ranking Secured Deposit from Orange Finance Ltd. Orange Finance has not made any loans to related parties but is 100 percent owned by Money Managers founder Doug Somers-Edgar . . . Doug Somers-Edgar has stopped accepting investments in his finance company Orange Finance but the company says it can repay investors on their expected maturity date . . . Covenant Trustee managing director Graeme Miller said Orange had indicated it could meet all its obligations as they fell due. That's despite the fact that a number of the company's loans were overdue, according to its September 2007 financial statements.

Notes

Chapter 3: Reality check: Who needs economic
growth anyway?

1   *OECD Factbook 2008.*
2   http://www.stats.govt.nz/products-and-services/Articles/
    unpaidwork-Jun01.htm.
3   http://imf.org/external/pubs/ft/weo/2008/02/weodata/index.aspx.
4   ttp://earthtrends.wri.org/searchable_db/index.php?theme=5.
5   *OECD Factbook 2008.*
6   Diener, E & Seligman, MEP, *Beyond Money – Toward an Economy of
    Well-Being*, American Psychological Society, 2004.
7   http://hdr.undp.org/en/reports/global/hdr2009/.
8   Diener, E & Seligman, MEP, *Beyond Money – Toward an Economy of
    Well-Being*, American Psychological Society, 2004.
9   http://www.treasury.govt.nz/publications/research-policy/
    wp/2005/05-09/02.htm.
10 http://www.worldvaluessurvey.org/.
11 http://www.american.com/archive/2008/may-june-magazine-
    contents/can-money-buy-happiness.
12 White, A (2007),'A Global Projection of Subjective Well-being: A
    Challenge To Positive Psychology?', *Psychtalk* 56, 17–20. The data
    on SWB and SWLS were extracted from a meta-analysis by Marks,
    Abdallah, Simms & Thompson (2006).
13 BM Friedman, *The Moral Consequences of Economic Growth*, Random
    House, 2005.
14 Lopez (2004),'Pro-Poor Growth: A Review of What We Know (and
    What We Don't)'.

Chapter 4: Our economy and the Kiwi obsession with property

1   Treasury Report, *A Synopsis of Theory, Evidence and Recent Treasury
    Analysis on Saving*, 2007.
2   OECD Compendium of Productivity Indicators 2008.

3 Treasury Working Paper 07/04, *Housing in the Household Portfolio and Implications for Retirement Saving: Some Initial Finding from SOFIE*, 2007.

4 Reserve Bank 2006.

5 http://www.interest.co.nz/ratesblog/index.php/2008/09/05/property-investing-boom-doubles-laqc-tax-losses/.

6 Connolly and Kohler (2004).

7 *NZ Herald*, 29 March 2009.

8 Dominick Stephens, 'Bubble, schmubble', *Westpac Economic Research*, 16 March 2007.

9 Carmen N Reinhart and Kenneth S Rogoff, *The aftermath of financial crises*, 2008.

Chapter 8: Seeking professional help — but getting stitched up

1 'The high cost of bad advice', *Sunday Star-Times*, 5 August 2007.

2 *Sunday Star-Times*, 30 September 2007.

Chapter 9: Independence Day

1 'The Hidden Sales Scandal', 12 August 2007.

2 *Financial Alert*, 7 April 2009.

Chapter 10: Regulatory sleepwalkers

1 http://fsahandbook.info/FSA/html/handbook/PRIN/2/1.

Acknowledgements

This book has benefited from an enormous amount of intelligence on portfolios and investment advisor behaviour supplied to me by the investing public — especially those who unfortunately have seen their wealth demolished and have come to us for help. It is a modern-day tragedy that these folk have seen their lifetime savings vaporise and yet those responsible are able to hide behind corporate logos and reinvent themselves to practise their alchemy again.

Within my own office the team has gathered an extensive amount of evidence and provided much of the economic analysis upon which the book is based. So to the team who have provided so much help — Jonathan Glass, Clint Van Marrewijk, Roger Browne, Chris Worthington, Geoff Simmons, Susan Easton, Robert Taylor and Andrew Gawith — I extend my sincere thanks.

Thanks to Ruby Morgan, who assisted with the research, and I am grateful to Bernard Hickey for his advice and wisdom. As usual John McCrystal has applied his magic to the writing to ensure it flows and I don't get bogged down in economics or investment-sector jargon and minutiae.

But all errors and omissions are my own, all responsibility for the evidence presented is my own, and none of those who have helped along the way, by bringing to my attention examples of the poor practices cited in this text, bear any responsibility for what I have said.

So many books try to expose bad behaviour and even worse practice but stop short of presenting specific examples. Despite the mass destruction to New Zealanders' wealth that the financial sector has wrought, the avenues of redress that ordinary folk have are so woefully inadequate that justice and accountability remain elusive. This reality is something our regulators should be ashamed of and it requires urgent redress if the individuals behind the offending companies are to be stopped from once again performing their tricks with impunity on another generation of Kiwi saving suckers.

Gareth Morgan